BORTHWICK INSTITUTE
UNIVERSITY OF YORK

Eric James and the Founding of the University of York

by

Allen Warren

BORTHWICK PAPER 126

First Published 2017

© Allen Warren 2017

ISSN: 0524-0913
ISBN: 978-1-904497-61-5

Eric as Vice-Chancellor

Acknowledgements

As with any work of this kind the author has had support and help from many individuals and institutions.

To the Sheldon Memorial Trust, I would like express gratitude for the invitation to deliver the original lecture. Initially, the hope was that it could be delivered by the late Professor Barrie Dobson, but sadly that was not possible. The lectures committee of the Trust has been unfailingly supportive.

In this connection I would like to record my thanks to the late Sir Donald Barron and his widow, Gillian. Sir Donald remained a member of the lectures committee until his death in late 2015 and had been associated with the evolution of the University since 1955, initially as Treasurer to the York Academic Trust, later as Treasurer and Chairman of the University Council and life-long supporter of the University as the Chairman of the Rowntree Company, the Midland Bank and as a member of the University Grants Committee. His remarkable insight, intelligence and memory inform a great deal of what follows about York, the City, Minster, University and its major company. It was a privilege to have known him.

To Professor Oliver James, Eric and Cordelia James' son, I owe a particular debt for his enthusiastic support and help especially in conversation and through making available family material and for permission to use the family's photographs.

A significant number of individuals helped with their own memories and assessments. For Eric's period as an assistant master at Winchester from 1933-1945, I would like to thank particularly the late Irvine and Major-General Stuart Watson, the late Sir Jeremy Morse, A.O.J. Cockshutt and the late Gerald Aylmer, who had attended the school in this period. For his time at Manchester Grammar School, I thank again A.O.J. Cockshutt, Mrs Ursula Aylmer, the late Dr. Penry Williams, Dr. Ivan Hall and those former staff and pupils who recorded their appreciations at the time of his leaving the school and his death, especially the writer Alan Garner.

For the York period, I give special thanks to Catherine West-Taylor, widow of the first Registrar, John, for information about her husband, his early life and education, especially in Cambridge, and for their friendships with Henry Morris and Stirrat Johnson-Marshall. Among the early staff members of the University I am indebted to David Foster, Mark Williamson, David and Isobel Waddington, Gordon Leff, Keith Robbins, William Thomas, Peter Rycraft, the late Roger and Ileana McMeeking and the late Norman and Jacqueline Hampson. Among the early students, I would like to thank Bill and Sarah Sheils, Jim Walvin and Chris Perry.

To the various libraries and archive and their staff, Chris Webb (Borthwick Institute for Archives, University of York), Clive Henly (the Old Vardeanian Association), Michael O'Riordain (Archivist to the Queen's College, Oxford), to Simon Bailey (University of Oxford Archives), Susan Foster (Archivist to Winchester College), Rachel Neale (Archivist to Manchester Grammar School), Peter Young (Archivist to York Minster). In addition, the staff of the J.B. Morrell Library, University of York, The National Archive, the Institute for Education, University of London, the British Library and Manchester University Library and Archives have all been unfailingly helpful.

For permissions to use published or photographic material in their copyright ownership, Leeds University Library, Manchester Grammar School, the University of York, the University of East Anglia, the Rowntree Foundation, the Nestlé Company, the National Portrait Gallery, the Wellcome Library, Getty Images, York Museums Trust, Professor Oliver James, Catherine West-Taylor, Bridget Nuttgens, David Foster and Mike Shales. I would particularly like to thank Paul Shields, the University photographer, for his help with the illustrations.

Any errors or omissions are the responsibility of the author.

The author gratefully acknowledges support from the Sheldon Memorial Trust in conducting the research underpinning the volume. Also to Chris Webb a supportive and patient editor.

Abbreviations

Note on James' manuscripts

Nearly all the material relating to James' own work as the founding Vice-Chancellor is located in the Borthwick Institute for Archives, based in the University of York. It includes the University's own Vice-Chancellors papers and James' personal and professional papers, which were deposited in the Borthwick by Cordelia, Lady James after her husband's death. A small quantity of material remains with the James family.

Biographical Notes

In a study of this kind, a large number of those involved took a prominent part in the public life of the period. Nearly all feature as entries in the Oxford Dictionary of National Biography, Who was Who or through an obituary in The Times. Some not included in any of these works of reference have entries on Wikipedia. All these reference sources can now be accessed on line and so, in order not to overburden the text, biographical information is only included if it contributes significantly to the text or is about a person not obviously known through these on line resources.

Appendices

The following study is not a comprehensive intellectual biography of Eric James, nor is it a full account of his career as an educationalist. Much more could be written about his time at Manchester and on the national educational stage in the years after 1945. Similarly, it does not analyse his later contributions to teacher training or to debates in the House of Lords, largely on social and educational issues.

But to understand the teacher, headmaster and vice-chancellor I decided to include some previously unstudied or private material that relates to Eric James' religious and moral positions combined with his belief in the role of science in improving human beings. Similarly, because he became so identified with a belief in selective education, I thought it useful to print for the first time his address to the Northern Heads conference in 1954, which lays out his views in the most robust style in the presence of Hugh Gaitskell and the Labour Party education front bench team of Michael Stewart and Alice Bacon, along with the extract from Gaitskell's own diary entry relating to the conference.

In the same way, I thought it would be helpful to include the full text of the bid of the University of York Promotion Committee to the UGC, making the case for a university in the city, written by John West-Taylor, and described by Sir Keith Murray, Chairman of the UGC, as a 'masterpiece'.

Once the case for a university at York had been accepted, the UGC appointed an Academic Planning Board, to oversee the process, beginning with the appointment of a Vice-Chancellor. Methods of making senior appointments have changed so dramatically over the last half century or so, I decided to outline the appointment is some detail as a case study in elite decision making in the 1950s.

Photographs and captions

Note: Many of the images are undated but roughly correspond to the person's age at the time being discussed in the text.

Cover

Derwent Court: watercolour by Patrick Nuttgens c.1980

Frontispiece

Eric as Vice-Chancellor

Preface

This study of the life and career in education of Eric James, Lord James of Rusholme, owes its origins to the kind invitation by the Sheldon Memorial Trust to give a lecture on Eric James in its series of annual lectures on citizens of the city of York who had a significant impact on the development of the city in the thirty years following the Second World War. It was delivered in the Merchant Adventurers' Hall in September 2013. Eric James was the founding vice-chancellor of the University of York and the lecture coincided with the 50th anniversary of the opening of the University in October 1963. The lecture was given in a more extended two lecture format in November of the same year in the University. The present volume is a more fully developed version of the content of those lectures.

The Sheldon Memorial Trust is dedicated to extending the understanding of the history and civic traditions of the city through education, lectures, seminars and publications. Prompted by the late Sir Donald Barron, a Trustee, the annual lectures were revived and to date have included lectures and publications on Oliver Sheldon himself, J.B. Morrell (businessman, civic leader and philanthropist), Hans Hess (pioneering post-war director of York City Art Gallery), and George Harris (Director and Chairman of the Rowntree Company). The careers and lives of these men were mainly within the life and economy of the city. Two other figures who, in different but complementary ways, made their impact on the city as the final stage of already distinguished careers in other cities. These were Eric Milner-White (Dean of York 1941 until his death in 1963, and formerly Dean of King's College, Cambridge 1918-1941) and Eric James (founding vice-chancellor of the University of York from 1961 until his retirement in 1973 and formerly High Master of Manchester Grammar School from 1945 until 1961).

In these two latter cases, the Trust decided that a different approach to publication of the lecture(s) should be followed, which in the case of Eric James has led to present volume, and in the case of Eric Milner-White was explored through a seminar on his life at the University of York's Festival of Ideas in June 2016.

The author decided that any analysis of Eric James' contribution to the founding and development of the University in the City could be best understood, firstly by bringing together an understanding of the life, character and career of the man, and secondly by studying how far the aspirations of the University of York Promotion Committee and those of the University Grants

Committee, as the principal funding body on behalf of the government, had been realised by the time of his retirement in 1973. What follows, therefore, is a combination of intellectual and professional biography with an analysis of the founding of a distinctive institution at a particular historical moment in twentieth century Britain.

Eric James and the Founding of the University of York[1]

On April 19th 1960 Sir Keith Murray, Chairman of the University Grants Committee, wrote to the Chairman of the York University Promotion Committee, Archbishop Michael Ramsey, that its recommendation to the Treasury to establish two new universities at Norwich and York had been accepted.[2] With this, the long campaign since 1946 to secure a university in the city had been won and planning could begin in earnest.

The founding of seven new universities from the late 1950s was a unique experiment in British higher education. Never before had a British government decided that the country needed more graduates, and that a proportion should be educated within wholly new national institutions that had been created for the contemporary world, uncluttered by existing practices and traditions. By implication, at least, the decision represented a frustration with the existing university 'system' and some of the attitudes it expressed.[3]

With this Treasury endorsement, the UGC moved quickly and, following the precedent used at Sussex, they formed an Academic Planning Board to oversee the establishing of the university at York. Made up of a group of the 'great and the good' and with some local representation and chaired by Lord Robbins, they met for the first time in October 1960 to begin the process of drawing up the Charter and Statutes and to appoint a founding Vice-Chancellor. For the latter, they solicited suggestions and within a month had created a list of some thirty five men. From this list they appear to have decided to invite a single nominee to York to visit the site on December 5th and a few days later to meet some of the Board members in London. That man was Eric, Lord James of Rusholme, then High Master of Manchester Grammar School. He asked for a month to consider the offer and on return from an educational visit to West Africa accepted, news that was received 'with enthusiasm' by the York University Promotion Committee. No other candidate seems to have been considered seriously. He formally took up the post on January 1st 1962.[4]

But before moving to analyse and describe Eric's role as founding Vice-Chancellor in more detail, two preliminary questions need to be asked. Why was the city of York one of the two preferred locations for the beginning of this national experiment of creating new universities? What was it about the case made by York that was more convincing than those of the other towns and cities also lobbying for their own university? Secondly, how far was the submission by the York University Promotion Committee sufficiently innovative and imaginative academically to convince Murray and his colleagues?[5] In other words, how far had the ethos, shape and purposes of a university at York been fashioned **before** James' appointment?

Taking the first question, and as is well known, there had been a group of individuals in York since 1945 who believed that York should possess a university. They included Oliver Sheldon, John Bowes Morrell, both men of York, and Eric Milner-White, Dean of York since 1941, and previously Dean of King's College, Cambridge.[6] In 1947 they had presented their case to the UGC, the body that had had oversight of the university system as a whole since the 1920s. York was not alone in making a pitch at that time. Among other applicants were Norwich and Brighton, but they also included places such as Gloucester and Carlisle. Significantly, in York's case, the lead had not been taken by the local authorities or any of the leading employers in the city, but by a collection of individuals.[7] As a group, their pride in York was not confined to the ambition to secure a university, but was part of a much wider process of civic renewal and an aesthetic belief in the uniqueness of the city, its buildings, heritage and their potential. This had led in the immediate post-war years to the founding of the York Civic Trust, the flourishing of the York Georgian Society and the revival of the city's livery companies, all expressions of a more generalised concern about how the city was going to respond to the climate of optimistic reconstruction following victory in Europe. More particularly, how were its historic buildings to be put to new use?

The UGC had received the submission in 1947 politely. Its chairman, Sir Walter Moberly, commented that it was more of an 'idea' than a plan. More relevantly, the UGC and therefore also the government did not think that new universities were needed. They believed any growth in demand from suitably qualified student applicants could be met through expanding existing universities or by granting full university status to the university colleges in Hull, Reading, Exeter and Leicester. Of course, the Committee continued, it was possible that this policy might change in the longer term with totally new locations being chosen on the basis in part of what quasi-university activity was already taking place there. York would need to show how it could meet such highly speculative criteria.[8]

The response was not exactly encouraging, but the York group did not give up and set about seeing what kind of quasi-university activity might be encouraged. They formed a committee of the Civic Trust to develop schemes and in 1951 selected a young Cambridge graduate, John West-Taylor, to be its secretary. This turned out to be a critically important appointment, although no one could have realised it at the time.[9] Progress in the early 1950s was slow but not unpromising. John West-Taylor as effectively director of the academic project and his colleagues did establish two academic institutes - The Institute of Advance Architectural Studies and the Borthwick Institute of Historical Research - each supplying a relevant new use for historic buildings in the city – respectively St John's Church, Ousegate, and St Anthony's Hall, Peasholme Green. Later they also acquired part of the King's Manor. Other potential developments floated across the horizon, with Eric Milner-White, the group's chairman, always imaginative and idealistic about what might be possible. Could York, for instance, find a single very wealthy donor to endow an individual college as Lords Nuffield and Wolfson were doing in Oxford and Cambridge; a college, which might be something akin to All Souls College, Oxford, but in the north of England, as a centre of scholarship and research in the arts, but without undergraduates? As the number of overseas participants in the IAAS courses grew, Milner-White in 1954 had the idea of a School for Britain, largely catering for this overseas interest in English architecture, history and the arts. Might York, alternatively, gradually become a centre for excellence through a cluster of in-service and professional institutes building upon the IAAS and the Borthwick. One such scheme that had considerable support was for a professional staff college for the local authorities to be based in the King's Manor. Harold Oldman, the Chief Education Officer for York, worked thoroughly on the idea. Advice was taken from Norman Fisher, the head of the National Coal Board Staff College and formerly Chief Education Officer for Manchester, as it was also from Sir Harold Banwell, a leading figure in the local authority world. The formidable Dame Evelyn Sharpe, the permanent secretary at the Ministry of Housing and Local Government, was said to be enthusiastic. For a while, it seemed that a staff college or a university might be rival schemes. More significant practically were the activities of J.B. Morrell, who always had an eagle-eye for real estate and its potential. Morrell also thought there was a better use for the King's Manor than as a staff college. Largely on his own initiative, he acquired the then unoccupied Heslington Hall and its surrounding grounds from the Deramore family, just seventeen acres on the south-east corner of the city, for some unspecified future civic use.[10]

Even so, by the mid-1950s the campaign to secure a university had become becalmed. The institutes were successfully established and capable of further additions and development, but the idea of them forming a core of a fledgling university seemed remote. As far as the UGC was concerned the national situation had not changed.[11] Gradual expansion could be incorporated within existing institutions. But from 1955 or 1956, the policy climate began to change. In the first place, assumptions about the numbers of suitably qualified young adults wishing to continue in education after the age of 18 rose sharply, driven by prosperity, rising ambitions and expectations along with a wider understanding of the scientific and technological needs of society.[12] At its meeting in November 1956 there was a wide ranging discussion, and in particular whether the arts should be included in any proposed growth in student numbers. For his part the then Sir Eric James, High Master of Manchester Grammar School, commented that the arts 'were not expanding subjects and the end of any profitable development in them might be in sight'. Disagreeing Sir George Clark, Provost of Oriel College, Oxford, supported the continuing expansion of the classics, while Sir George Thomson, Master of Corpus Christi College, Cambridge, expressed doubts that foreign language degrees had the same value as others in developing the mind of the student.[13]

Not that York was likely to benefit obviously from such a change in policy on university expansion. Science had never featured in the thinking of Milner-White, John Bowes Morrell and their associates. This was perfectly understandable given the power and reputation of the University of London and the big civic universities in science and engineering. Their most visionary thoughts had concentrated on the arts at both undergraduate and postgraduate level. There was a possibility of including the social sciences in order to build on the resources and traditions of the Rowntree Trusts, most probably in areas of social practice, professional development and in-service training.[14] Milner-White, as chairman of what was now an independent York Academic Trust, was in contact with Murray in the autumn of 1958 through John West-Taylor and Norman Fisher seeking support and endorsement for the degree level programmes in the two institutes. He was pretty despondent with Murray's reply even though it seemed very likely that a single new university would be founded in Sussex.[15] Wholly new universities were regarded by the UGC and their Treasury pay-masters as expensive and complicated projects, particularly in small urban centres in relation to the supply of student accommodation, where lodgings would be difficult to find in sufficient numbers.

Then quite suddenly a few months after Milner-White had contacted the UGC, the whole atmosphere changed.[16] John West-Taylor as secretary to the York Academic Trust had remained the one person, whose eyes had remained firmly on the long-term objective, a full university in York. Indeed that was the reason he had applied in 1951 for the relatively modest position of secretary, from which he had worked to establish the IAAS in particular. Widely networked, he had heard indirectly through Sir Herbert Read, then President of the York Philosophical Society, that the government may have had a change of heart. His informant was the same Norman Fisher.[17] John made an informal enquiry of Murray in December 1958.[18] The response on this second occasion was very different; that the UGC and the Treasury were now minded to establish a number of wholly new universities in addition to Sussex, probably two in the first instance. The reasons for this change in government thinking are not easy to pin down without more research within the machinery of government as the Macmillan administration moved into re-election mode early in 1959. But within the UGC membership, and including Murray in particular, there was an increasing frustration with what was seen as the unresponsive, unimaginative world of the big civic universities.[19] Direct encouragement to expand had been met by procrastination especially within arts faculties, where the opinion of 'more means worse' was widely held. Difficulties were made about potential urban sites and how expansion would be funded? Murray and his colleagues concluded that civic universities had become places in which learning only happened between nine and five, using sterile teaching methods and within faculties that were dominated by professors, all stifling creativity and imagination.[20]

In this changed political environment, Murray told West-Taylor that if York wished to be considered as a potential new university town then it would have to prepare a scheme quickly, not just a vision, to compete with other centres, most notably Norwich which was now ahead of the game. West-Taylor acted swiftly and Murray was invited to come to York in June 1959 for an informal set of conversations at Bishopthorpe Palace under the eye of Archbishop Ramsay, who had agreed to head a modified Academic Trust in preparing a scheme. Murray agreed, staying overnight with Milner-White, and meeting the small York deputation the following morning.[21] He was also taken to view the Heslington estate from the high ground by the water tower, which, unlike Eric's visit eighteen months later on a damp December day, was a master-stroke. Murray commented on what he saw as a wonderful environment for a university:

> 'The lawns and trees give a very gracious setting – a very important factor.'[22]

More practically, West-Taylor had prepared detailed briefing notes for those attending the meeting at Bishopthorpe earlier in the day. He concluded, 'This is probably York's best and last chance.'[23]

These notes became the core document prepared for the formal meeting with the UGC in London at the end of 1959, and which Murray described as 'a masterpiece'. Once the UGC had given the go-ahead in April 1960 this same document was the basis for the newly formed Academic Planning Board's discussions leading to its own Interim Report to the University of York Promotion Committee, still chaired by the Archbishop in March 1961, just a few weeks after James had accepted the post of incoming Vice-Chancellor. Therefore to answer the first question – there was an articulate vision and outline plan already prepared for the new university as Eric James was appointed and with which he was happy to work and realise.

One of the real bonuses in doing the research on Eric James and the University of York is to discover the critical role played by John West-Taylor. Not only is this confirmed by the documents making the case to the UGC and their importance, but also in the universal testimony of James, Andrew Derbyshire, the University's founding architect, and Dr. Patrick Nuttgens, the Director of the Institute of Advanced Architectural Studies from 1961 in a series of interviews conducted in the early 1980s by the architectural historian, Andrew Saint, now deposited in the British Library.[24]

John West-Taylor had been an undergraduate at Cambridge, after service in the Fleet Air Arm. He had become interested in social and community architecture and had been taken up by Henry Morris, not himself a don, but who had been Chief Education Officer for Cambridgeshire since 1922. Morris was the son of a plumber from Lancashire; educated at elementary school, he had initially begun training for the Anglican ministry in Wales. Frustrated by its provincialism, he found his way to Oxford University, saw service in the First World War, finally going to King's College, Cambridge, graduating in philosophy. Charismatic, dogmatic, aesthetic, friendly, impossible, he began a career as a local authority bureaucrat in the education department of Cambridgeshire County Council. Within months, owing to the death of his boss, he became Chief Education Officer of one of the poorest rural authorities in England, a post he then held for thirty two years. By the time John met him, Morris had secured a world-wide reputation through a pioneering vision of 'community education' through his Cambridgeshire Village Colleges. These replaced the poorly resourced and managed church and local authority elementary schools with institutions providing a comprehensive community service in relation to education, culture and social life. Central to his vision was the provision of fine quality buildings, pleasant and stimulating internal decoration with interesting art work, set in carefully managed grounds. Morris was one of the great chief education officers for local authorities, a group of men for whom the 1944 Education Act was an inspiring enactment, giving the possibility of a transformative educational system from the age of primary school through to university and beyond.[25] John came to know Morris well, taking lodgings in his house in Fitzwilliam Street and later becoming his travelling companion. Through this connection John, and later his wife Catherine, came to know architects also influenced by Morris including the public building architects' practice of Robert Matthew Johnson-Marshall, subsequently chosen as architects by the fledgling University of York.[26]

What do these documents submitted to the UGC tell us about the vision of John West-Taylor and his colleagues within the York Academic Trust, which won the case for a university and then framed its early development by the team led by Eric James?

Firstly, they show the critical importance of the change in the thinking of the UGC and the government about 'new universities' in 1958 and 1959, a period which also encompassed the re-election of the Macmillan government in October 1959. As far as York as a potential location was concerned, this meant the active support and encouragement of Sir Keith Murrray personally. As a result the York Academic Trust had to develop a very different educational project, elements of which had never been part of any earlier thinking. This new university proposal had to include the physical sciences, it was to engage in undergraduate and postgraduate studies, it was to award its own degrees from the beginning, it was to be innovative and focus on undergraduate teaching, it was to be seen as a national, not simply a local or specialist institution, and it was to anticipate a size of at least 2000 students over time.

Secondly, John West-Taylor was critical in developing that case, in both preparing for the meetings at Bishopthorpe and later in London in December 1959, and by his support for Milner-White and Archbishop Ramsey in securing public endorsement from within the city and county. If we study the content

Sir Keith Murray

Lord Robbins

Henry Morris

John West-Taylor

Oliver Sheldon

J.B. Morrell

Dean Eric Milner-White

William Wallace

Archbishop Michael Ramsey

of these documents in detail, we see the subsequent form of the university in outline – relatively traditional academic disciplines, but excluding applied sciences, medicine and law, a commitment to undergraduate tutorial teaching and to innovation within the curriculum, an ambition to reconcile specialist subject understanding with a broader informed literacy, a more democratic academic and institutional structure of governance, and finally a commitment to research, professional development and in-service training through a structure of institutes. What was not explicitly included at the outset was the desire that the university should be collegiate in structure. This was not an element in the discussions at Bishopthorpe, but it was present later in the year at the formal meeting with the UGC in December. This may have been a prudent omission on the earlier occasion, since conventional thinking at the time still saw students living in lodgings for most of their undergraduate careers, and that the costs of a residential collegiate university were likely to be considerable. It was expressed, however, as an aspiration and it is not unreasonable to assume that this element came from Milner-White, for whom the collegiate model as reflected in his twenty years as Dean of King's College, Cambridge was a lyrical memory. It is also likely to have been supported by John West-Taylor.

Thirdly, the role of Lord Robbins in chairing the York Academic Planning Board, in the appointment of Lord James and in producing the Interim Report, which subsequently became the Development Plan, was also of vital importance. Robbins appears very early in Murray's thinking and that of the UGC as a potential Chairman of such a Board, should the Treasury agree to establishing a university in York. Robbins, who had been created a life peer in the same cohort as Eric James, was also a man at the centre of the state establishment at this time. Professor of Economics at the London School of Economics since 1929, he epitomised the 'great and the good' and it is no surprise that he should be on any UGC list of potential chairman of Academic Planning Boards. But it is not simply coincidence that he was nominated for York.[27]

At this point another character comes into play that was to have a significant influence on the early shape of the university and especially in the field of the social sciences. Again now largely forgotten, his name is William Wallace. Born in 1891 Wallace had trained as a solicitor. After non-combatant service in the First World War, he had joined the Rowntree Company in 1919. He spent his entire career with the company becoming its chairman in 1952 and retiring in 1957. A man of scholarly interests in economics and applied social sciences, he had written articles on private enterprise and the state's role in business. Liberal in politics, he had written the text of Lloyd George's manifesto in the 1929 general election, *We can conquer unemployment*, something he only made public many years later. Approaching retirement in late 1956, he had joined the York Academic Trust and had also become chairman of the Joseph Rowntree Memorial Trust.

He quickly became active in the campaign for a university, joining the delegation to make the formal presentation to the UGC in London in December 1959. Given that the significance of Rowntree Trusts was an important element in York's case for a university, Wallace was an influential and powerful figure, whose character has been described as 'aggressive in a gentlemanly way.'[28]

Wallace was in contact directly with Murray once the decision to found a university had been made, pressing for the appointment of Robbins as Chairman of the Academic Planning Board. Robbins would be the link between the world of Murray and the UGC and that of the Rowntree Trusts, having himself recently joined the Joseph Rowntree Social Services Trust (JRSST), whose chairman was J.B. Morrell. On his own initiative, Wallace invited Robbins in his role as a member of the JRSST to attend the meeting of his own Trust, the Joseph Rowntree Memorial Trust, on 30 September. By this point Wallace was also a member of the JRSST and made it clear that substantial additional sums might be released from the Joseph Rowntree Memorial Trust to support the social sciences in the nascent university. He also nominated Lord James to the Board for consideration as the first Vice-Chancellor. Later in the year, and before Eric was appointed, Wallace had submitted to the Academic Planning Board his own outline proposals for the Social Sciences at York.

Alongside this public interest in the case for a university, Wallace had a personal interest which led him to a long and slightly embarrassing correspondence with Robbins on whether Wallace's professional and scholarly writings might be submitted as the material for the award of a PhD from the London School of Economics. Robbins was not encouraging. Later Wallace lobbied the founding Head of the Economics Department, Alan Peacock, who described him as making a 'determined' effort to influence how economics was taught at York. This antagonised Eric, who regarded it as illegitimate interference. Unlike Lloyd Owen, his successor as Chairman of the Rowntree Company, Wallace was never invited to join the University Council.[29]

In conclusion therefore, the founders of the University of York were a collection of individuals and interests in York and London, who had the inspiration to want to secure a university in the city, and who were able in 1959 quickly to develop a convincing and worked-up proposal, which had been accepted by the government, along with a similar proposal from the city of Norwich. They were to be the first in an, as yet, unspecified programme of university expansion. It was the same group of individuals and interests who charged James to realise their proposal by adding his own distinctive imprint.

Who then was the man Michael Ramsey reported his committee as appointing with 'enthusiasm' early in 1961? James' entry in *Who's Who* for 1961 reads,

> James of Rusholme, Baron, cr.1959, of Fallowfield (Life Peer), Eric John Francis James, Kt.1956; High Master of Manchester Grammar School since 1945; b.1909; yr.s.of F.W.James; m.1939, Cordelia, d.of late Major-General F. Wintour, C.B., C.B.E.; one s.
>
> Educ; Taunton's Sch., Southampton; Queen's College, Oxford [Exhibitioner and Honorary Scholar, 1927, Hon. Fellow, 1959], Goldsmiths' Exhibitioner, 1929; B.A. [1st Class Hons., Chemistry], B.Sc.1931; M.A., D.Phil, 1933; Asst.Master at Winchester College, 1933-1945; Member of the University Grants Committee, 1949-58; Chairman of the Headmasters' Conference 1953-54; Mem. Central Advisory Council on Education, 1957; Member Standing Commission on Museums and Galleries, 1958, Hon.LL.D [McGill] 1957. Publications: [in part] Elements of Physical Chemistry; [in part] Science and Education; An Essay on the Content of Education; Education and Leadership; articles in scientific and educational journals. Address: The Grammar School, Manchester 13; Club: Athenaeum.

Background and Education

At first reading, therefore, appointed by the 'great and the good', Eric James was one of the 'club'. His demeanour and appearance at that time would have confirmed such an impression. Formal dress, Homberg hat, a deep booming, curiously accent-less voice with the habit of doing business in the Athenaeum.[30] But such impressions can be misleading.

Eric's father, Francis, was a commercial traveller in brushes, who had

moved with his mother, Lily, a governess before her marriage, from West
Ham to Derby sometime during the first decade of the twentieth century.
Eric's brother and sister had both been born in West Ham and were nine
and seven years older than him. Eric's father was 45 and his mother was 38
when he was born. So his early family life was probably quite solitary, not
exactly an only child of elderly parents, but with some elements of that. They
do not seem to have been part of a wide or close family network, perhaps
because of Frank's frequent changes of place of work and there is little
reference in family memory to aunts, uncles and cousins. Also, the world of
the commercial traveller was a pretty varied one for much of the twentieth
century, ranging from the world of spivs and sharp dealers to that of serious,
hard-working, respectable vendors of goods and services. Frank James was
undoubtedly in the latter category. The family's terraced house in White
Street, Derby was reasonably spacious, accommodating his mother in law as
well as a maid, something that was typical in the street. But it was an insecure
world, hence the frequent moves; it was outside the professions, money was
hard-earned and disaster was always possible. It was also a world of social as
well as financial nervousness in which appearances were important as well as
ambition for the children. The James parents were devout non-conformists,
almost certainly Congregationalists. Frank was a bookish man, a taste fully
passed on to Eric, and Lilian's experience as a governess probably created a
disciplined family atmosphere. Certainly, in Oliver James' words, there were,
'no frivolities'.[31]

We know little about Eric's early years before he is recorded aged ten
attending Brighton Municipal Secondary School for Boys, later renamed
Varndean School, and as living in Waterloo Street, Hove and later at 55
Miller's Road, Brighton. In about 1970 as a Vice-Chancellor and Life Peer,
Eric attended a professional meeting at Varndean School and chose to give a
verbal portrait himself at the school, which he described as a 'grand' school
which he had enjoyed. He speculated that his school report might have been
expressed as follows - Attainment A, Industry B, Neatness and Personal
Appearance C. He described himself as like a character drawn by Ronald
Searle, one whose hair always needed cutting and whose 'subcutanaceous
glands secreted ink'.[32] By 1923 Eric's family had moved again to Southampton,
with his father now 'a commercial jeweller'. Eric, clearly a clever little boy,
now enrolled at Taunton's School. It is not known whether his father paid
or whether he had a local authority scholarship. Founded in the eighteenth
century by a successful Southampton wine trader, as a school for local boys,

it had gradually became a public secondary school during the late nineteenth century, changing its name in 1910 from Taunton's Trade School to Taunton's School. Almost all its capital funds came from the public purse and a quarter of the pupils' fees were paid by the local education authority directly.[33]

We know little about Eric's time at the school either from the record or from his later conversation, except that he did become deputy Head Boy. But he did well and also was extremely fortunate. By being an endowed municipal school and because The Queen's College, Oxford had possessed lands in Southampton, the school had two exhibitions to the College exclusively for its pupils with the ability to gain entry. Eric was awarded one of these Southampton exhibitions worth £100. In addition he also won a town council award of £50 and a £15 bursary from the Stapley Trust. Eric's final school report survives and shows even then the impact he was making:

> James has completed a remarkably creditable school career and my colleagues feel very confident that he has a brilliant career ahead before him.[34]

So through academic ability, family support and luck, Eric James, who on any normal basis at the time might have been expected to enter a skilled or clerical trade on leaving school, went up in the autumn of 1927 to one of the leading universities in the world.

The Queen's College, Oxford, situated on the High Street next to All Souls and opposite University College, was not one of the grander Oxford Colleges, but it was quite wealthy for its size with about 200 students in total. It also had a larger number of exhibitions and scholarships than most, almost a third of its annual intake. The majority of these were awarded to boys from northern grammar schools, the Southampton exhibitions being the exception. Eric, therefore, was unlikely to have felt socially uncomfortable in the way that some scholarship boys did in more socially exclusive colleges, such as Christ Church.[35]

On his admission in October 1927, the College could well have been seen by freshmen as a gerontocracy. The Provost, John Richard McGrath, was almost 90, having been originally elected Provost in 1878. He continued to enjoy the fruits of his office, but in 1922 the Reverend E.M.Walker had been appointed pro-Provost. Eric later commented that the undergraduates put it about that the Provost was actually dead and that, like Bentham's, his body was simply wheeled out once a year.[36] Eric's tutor and later doctoral supervisor, Dr. F.D.Chattaway was also elderly, having been born in 1860.[37] But these appearances were deceptive. Chattaway was a distinguished organic chemist and a Fellow of the Royal Society, and the College as a whole was experiencing a golden period in terms of academic results and success in inter collegiate sport. In the finals examinations in 1930 twelve pupils secured first class honours degrees, including John Newsom, later described by Eric as a life-long friend[38]. In 1931 Eric was among six firsts in final university examinations and six in moderations, university exams taken in the first or second year. In the following year eight firsts were achieved, and in 1933 the College secured more firsts than any other college.[39]

We have two intriguing insights into Eric, the undergraduate chemist. The first is contained in the Vice-Provost's undergraduate interview book in which he recorded his meeting with Eric and his contemporaries along with their individual answers to a standard list of questions. Here Eric is described as playing chess for the university, not a sportsman and not liking music, thinking of becoming a teacher and, more intriguingly, as interested in Russian novels. There is no record of him playing any part in the life of the Junior Common Room, but he did participate in debating and literary societies. Even at this early stage we see someone combining interests in science and the arts. The remark about teaching is actually less revealing. After reading all entries in the record book for that year, a high proportion of the scholars, boys from non-privileged backgrounds, said that they were thinking about a teaching career. It was a main road for those making their way out of their modest family backgrounds through academic ability. At this point one might be forgiven for seeing Eric in one's mind's eye as a serious and cerebral young man, focussing on his books and his laboratory work, but the photographic evidence suggests someone also having a good time.[40]

As graduation approached in 1931, the question of career direction became more urgent. Eric later stated that he would have liked to have become a doctor, but his family would not have been able to pay for medical school. So like many before him and since, he made the trek to see the University Appointments Board. He was to do the same two years later. Again the notes of these interviews survive. In 1930 the interviewer comments, 'Grammar School type, but speaks well', queries whether he has an accent or not, and that he was 'neat and presentable'. He concluded, 'Probably an able chemist, suitable for day school or minor public school'. His tutor had commented 'a very good man and ought to get a first'.[41]

On graduation in 1931, Eric had essentially two choices – to become a schoolmaster or to become an industrial chemist as the two other Queen's chemistry scholars did in that year. In the event, the College, possibly for the first time, provided Eric with a post-graduate studentship in organic chemistry to work under Chattaway in the field of amide condensations. He completed his doctorate in two years in July 1933, having had a paper published with Chattaway in the Proceedings of the Royal Society the previous year.[42] His doctoral examiners, I.M.Heilbron and D. Hammick, both Fellows of the Royal Society noted,

> The thesis forms a definite and valuable contribution to the subject of amide condensations. It is presented in a most admirable and clear manner.....Mr James was examined orally and showed a very competent knowledge of the subject.[43]

It is likely that these two years were ones of considerable personal as well as academic development for Eric. A scholarly, non-sporty grammar school boy reading chemistry at Oxford in that period is likely to have matured more cautiously than some of his more privileged contemporaries; friendships more slowly made, especially with girls. Academic success had provided a personal platform from which to branch out, even if it did not resolve the question of career choice. Evidence of this survives in the tone and content of the notes made by the same interviewer at the Oxford University Appointments Board in 1933. Now they are very different:

> a tall, nice man (helped me over a point of geography) with keen interests in literature, art and music and well worth a public school post.

But just to remind ourselves that this was the Oxford of 1933, the interviewer also added in code on the record ' NTS', which being translated meant, 'Not Top Shelf'.[44]

Dr. Chattaway had also changed the tone of his comments to:
> Quite an outstanding man, will get his D.Phil....excellent teacher [he had been doing some demonstrating]. Ought to go to a really good p[ublic] s[chool].[45]

Winchester College 1933-1945

With this kind of academic endorsement, Eric applied for a temporary post in physics at Winchester College, a post subsequently confirmed, but more appropriately in chemistry. Eric later said that the only reason for his appointment was that the Head, the Reverend Alwyne Williams, simply did not know the difference between chemistry and physics. What is more likely is that Williams had seen in Eric a potentially able science teacher for a school that valued individual talent in its teaching staff almost more than any other.[46] Despite his Oxford education and now aged twenty four, Eric probably knew little in detail of the character of a leading public school like Winchester, whose staff had an almost unique self-assurance about its liberal individualism and encouragement of talent of all sorts. Along with its private school slang, its links with its richly endowed fellow foundation at New College, Oxford, and its record of state service from the days of its founder, William of Wykeham, in the fourteenth century, it knew it was good. It followed no nationally validated curriculum, boys progressed not by age but by ability or achievement, and public examinations were treated lightly given that its own examination system was sufficient to get into Oxford and Cambridge.[47] Eric remained at Winchester for twelve years and it was undoubtedly one of the formative experiences of his life, leading him much later to sending his own son to the College. But he also commented later that he had been somewhat 'intoxicated' by that first posting, seeing more faults in the school from the perspective of the 1980s than he had done fifty years before.[48]

The years at Winchester show a number of important features that would characterise Eric's future career. Almost immediately he found himself an outstanding teacher of chemistry, widely acknowledged by pupils. Despite being a co-author of one published research paper, Eric never considered an academic or research career. According to his son, Oliver, Eric saw himself as a good chemist but not an outstanding one. This is a remark which fits well with his later attitude as Vice-Chancellor in which he was sceptical about the value of much contemporary academic research, except the most creative and ground breaking.[49]

In the preface to his collected essays, *The Scientist as Rebel* (2006), dedicated to Eric and Cordelia James, the physicist Freeman Dyson writes about Eric, who had just died, and who had taught him at Winchester. His subversive teaching style reminded Dyson of the teacher in the contemporary film, *The Dead Poets Society* (1992). From the perspective of the classroom and the war-time harvest camps run by Eric and Cordelia James, he continues,

Like the teacher in the film, Eric James has a passion for poetry. He had a Ph.D.[sic], but he understood that it made no sense to bore us with formal lectures about chemical reactions which we could learn about much quicker from textbooks. So he put aside the ferrous and ferric oxides and read us the latest poems of Auden and Isherwood and Dylan Thomas and Cecil Day-Lewis, the poets who were then speaking for the younger generation in the first desperate years of World War Two......Eric remained at heart a rebel. Through forty years of active and creative life he remembered the sadness and the passion of the 1940s when we saw Hell break out on Earth.....That sadness and that passion are what made Eric a great teacher. The life of Eric James demonstrates that there is no contradiction between a rebellious spirit and an uncompromising pursuit of excellence in a rigorous intellectual discipline.[50]

That Eric was able to teach like this was not because Winchester allowed intelligent chaos to rule, rather it was because many masters acted also as what were called Div Dons, men usually teaching in the division of their subject, but who also took their own form in English, History and Divinity and for whom the pupil also had to write a weekly essay and receive a tutorial upon it. Within that framework, the master could broadly teach what he liked. Such a system allowed that widening of Eric's perspective and interests, noted in his final years at Oxford, to blossom. Thus the founding head of the University of York's history department, Gerald Aylmer, who had been a pupil of Eric's at Winchester within the science division, and who also shared Eric's religious non-belief, could later describe his lessons on the Minor Prophets as a 'revelation'.[51]

Another element in Eric's presence at Winchester was his participation in the College's Debating Society, of which he was later President. For instance, in October 1933, a month after arriving, Eric contributed to the debate on the motion that education should be based on the study of natural science.[52] Denying that scientists were blind to beauty, he continued that the pleasures of science were no different from any other intellectual pleasure, concluding 'Science goes deeper than test tubes; it is impossible to lightly dismiss, for it is in the bed and fabric of our life.' Seven years later in December 1940, Eric proposed the motion that 'this House attaches no value to the aristocracy', concluding 'The day of the privileged class was over in these days of democratisation.'[53]

Another critical event of the Winchester years was Eric's marriage to Cordelia Wintour on April 11th 1939. Up until that point, Eric had lived in a shared bachelors' house with two or three others, universally known as the 'rough house'. By his marriage, Eric's world widened further socially and culturally. Cordelia's father had been a successful soldier, veteran of late Victorian campaigns and the Great War. It was an intriguing and talented upper class world, a long way from the world of provincial nonconformist piety and practice. Cordelia herself had secured a first class honours degree in classical 'Greats' at Lady Margaret Hall, Oxford. Her brother, Charles, was to become a famous and pioneering journalist, editor of the Evening Standard in the late 1950s, and a life-long friend of Eric Hobsbawm, while her niece, Anna Wintour, became the long-term editor of Vogue in New York and was at one time tipped as a possible US ambassador to London. It was a sophisticated, metropolitan and not wholly conventional world with links into the socialist intelligentsia, so fully represented by Old Wykehamists like Hugh Gaitskell, Dick Crossman and Douglas Jay, all of whom had been at the College in the 1920s. Not that the James' marriage was in any way unconventional. Cordelia devoted herself selflessly to Eric's career, family and welfare, expressing her commitments through social action, the magistracy and with a directness about the local ecclesiastical hierarchy that made some blench. Anyone could see that they were a wonderful partnership and it is an amusing insight into their early married life to read of Eric leading harvesting camps during the war, with Cordelia and other wives doing the camp cooking.[54]

The final aspect of the Eric's experience at Winchester is what could be called the apprentice headmaster and educationalist. Eric was not a sportsman, nor did he serve long enough to become a housemaster, and Winchester did not appoint departmental heads in this period. He remained without disparagement an assistant master, the title of staff to this day. Critical to his development and his future career was the appointment of a new Headmaster in 1935, Spencer Leeson, at that time Headmaster of Merchant Taylors' School. A Wykehamist himself, Leeson was not simply returning to enjoy the College's distinguished traditions but to use its fame as a powerful force in the national debate about the future of education in Britain. This debate had begun before 1939, but gathered pace as the war progressed and the post-war world was planned in terms of full employment, education, health and comfortable old age. Leeson had a vision which Eric came to share, which had at its core a belief that the whole education system, independent, selective and maintained should have a nation-wide coherence.[55] Within these educational discussions,

Leeson, who was Chairman of the Headmasters' Conference throughout the war, had become the most powerful Headmaster in the country. In 1942, for instance, he persuaded the Winchester Fellows (governors) to pioneer a scheme in Hampshire and Hertfordshire whereby able boys would receive local authority bursaries to attend leading academic boarding as well as day schools. As a scheme it was endorsed in 1944 by a government report chaired by Lord Fleming, but R.A.Butler, as President of the Board of Education, characteristically declined to take on the more traditional and entrenched interests within the public school system. Consequently, it did not become a key element in the later 1944 Education Act.[56]

Leeson and Eric clearly had lengthy conversations about post-war education and each brought his own distinctive contribution to those conversations. Eric was a scientist, bringing an empirical rationalism to thinking about social, as well as moral, religious and political questions. He had not been a political ideologue in the world of conflicting opinions in the late 1930s. A significant number of his colleagues were socialists, often influencing their pupils in radical directions, especially during the Spanish Civil War with some later volunteering on the republican side. Eric remained radically inclined with Fabian inclinations. But principally he was 'the scientist as rebel' in Freeman Dyson's phrase, someone who found Hitler dangerous and subversive, but not himself becoming part of the left-wing drift in intellectual circles that could enthuse about Stalin's Russia in an uncritical way.[57] For Eric, a vision for the future was about science and technology and how it might be mobilised for human betterment. The range and quantity of science teaching was increasing at Winchester, but it by no means rivalled the traditional pre-eminence of the classical curriculum, in which Leeson had been schooled. As early as March 1940 and before the fall of France, Eric gave the first talk among the hundreds across his career to the Winchester Common Room. Entitled *Education and a Scientific Humanism*, it is a passionate advocacy of the importance and value of the teaching of science in schools for the nation's future. In it he explicitly used the vocabulary of the need to 'build a new Jerusalem' in the post-war world, which will have been seen as a long way off during the phoney war. It is included as Appendix 1.[58] This commitment was also fully expressed in the short volume, *Science and Education,* which Eric wrote with his older science colleague, E.M. Humby, published in 1942.[59] Leeson certainly thought highly of Eric. So, when the governors of Manchester Grammar School advertised for a new Highmaster in early 1945, he fully supported and possibly prompted Eric's application, as he did also for another member of his staff, Francis King. Some forty candidates applied and five were ultimately shortlisted, three serving Headmasters and the two assistant masters from Winchester. Eric, the youngest, secured the job aged 36.[60] But it is Leeson's report to his own governing body that is the most remarkable. In recording the comings and goings of staff, he comments on Eric's move, 'No wiser appointment could have been made. Dr James' especial strength did not so much lie in chemistry – although he was a brilliant student and teacher – as in his championship of a humane educational ideal'.[61] For his part, Eric on departing asked Leeson how he might be a successful Headmaster, a request that prompted a multi-page guidebook to headmastership, a text that Eric used verbatim when he became the leading headmaster of his day, but never passing it off as his own.[62]

As we move into the full-tide of Eric's professional life in September 1945 at Manchester, York and on a national stage, it is worth noting Sir Jeremy Morse's much later comment. Although he had not been taught by Eric, while a pupil himself at Winchester during the later stages of the War, one could not be unaware of his 'presence'.[63] In looking at Eric's achievements across his career as a whole, it is worth keeping in mind this quality in particular in a man about to become one of the youngest headmasters of a leading school. An inspiring teacher, a passionate scientific optimist, a believer in rational and informed progress, combined with a commitment to a humane educational ideal, and possessing 'presence'- the intangibles of leadership and vision.

Manchester Grammar School 1945-1962

By moving to Manchester just a few months after the end of the War and as the 1944 Education Act had passed into law, Eric moved with one step onto a national stage. His impact on the school itself was immediate, and along with his growing public reputation, an assumption arose that the prestige and eminence of the school was uniquely his achievement. This was reinforced by the prominence given in the 'high-brow' press at the time to academic results as measured by the number of Open Awards won to the universities of Oxford and Cambridge, the only league table of the period, and where Manchester Grammar School regularly took first place.[64] But this is misleading. M.G.S. was already a highly successful school, winning over forty university awards in the year prior to Eric's appointment. Nor was Eric a radical head – the curriculum evolved in a scientific direction, but classics and the liberal arts remained very strong. Sport also was sustained but not over-emphasised and the innovations introduced by other 'great' high master, J.L. Paton, following World War One, of outdoor education, Camp and Trek, were fully supported.[65] There were, for instance, five Scout troops in the school in the 1950s. In many ways, his most substantial contribution to the school came from his realisation that the 1944 Education Act, and the Direct Grant Grammar School system in particular, would change the whole context of an academic education in the city and region. With the provision of universal secondary education for the first time, Eric saw that the numbers of boys able and wishing to continue their education beyond the age of 15 and on to university would rise rapidly. He understood that facilities and staffing in the school would have to respond to those new challenges.[66] It is a better and more representative sign of the school's success by the mid-1950s that some 75% of all boys went on to university, that 58% of the sixth form, now totalling 460 out of a school of 1340, had studied mathematics and the sciences, and that over 100 boys left to study science and technology at university.[67]

In fact, Eric's impact on the school itself, pupils and staff, was more directly personal – that 'presence' that Jeremy Morse identified. There are many testimonies, but an early sign of what was to come was how the new High Master was known. For most, familiar but respectful nick-names come later, but in Eric's case, he was universally known within weeks by masters and boys alike as simply 'the Chief'. In his advice to Eric on headmastership, Leeson had concluded that above all he should possess the slightly enigmatic quality of 'incommunicable zest'.[68] Zest was a quality that the 36 year old Eric had in plenty.

Oliver Corbett, who taught classics at the school, described it from the perspective of a young member of staff:

> For some he was too good to be true; others thought him a human relations machine, an exemplification of text book management, who certainly compelled our respect and good will, but only won our affection by many acts of kindness and consideration and by his devotion and pride in M.G.S. For these were genuine and underlay the extraordinary mix of tact and directness, the desire to please, the love of an audience and the desire to play to the gallery, which doubtless repelled some, but welded those who liked it into a powerful combination.[69]

As for the pupils:

> Some found James distant, even cold and remote, but on others
> he left an indelible mark, especially those whom he taught chemistry
> and, memorably, humanities. The supreme reward of being ...
> [a pupil] at M.G.S. was to be taught by Eric James...The Fabian
> agnostic took upon himself the Religious Instruction of the Sixth
> Form. What we got was an awesome trip through the history of
> Western Thought, after a thorough grounding in Platonism, 'the
> Chief' bemoaning the while his ignorance of Classical Greek.[70]

For those being taught chemistry:

> He swept into the classroom like God descending from Mount
> Olympus and began to despatch the thunderbolts of Jove. In one
> particular lesson, he covered the whole blackboard with symbols,
> end groups and arrows and announced at the end of 45 minutes, that
> he had done the whole of the syllabus and that we simply had to
> reproduce the map. He then swept out as though with a puff of blue
> smoke.[71]

For other pupils, Alan Garner's experience is again revealing. Loitering in the
corridor and asked what he was doing, the young Garner had the quickness
to reply, 'Thinking, Sir.' Equally swiftly the tone changed instantly, 'Good.
Forgive the intrusion.' The same former pupil continued, 'I do not miss him.
What he was, in the effect he had on the boys of his High Mastership, and
what they passed on to the world, he still is and will be. He gave us our selves.
I can think of no greater gift.'[72]

Alongside this dynamic impact on Manchester Grammar School was
Eric's developing reputation as a public intellectual in the field of education
and his commitment to the vision informing the 1944 Education Act. With
the effective exclusion of the independent schools from the legislation, the
place of the Direct Grant Grammar Schools became a critical element with
Eric as its main public evangelist. Tony Cockshut, a pupil at Winchester
during the war, master at M.G.S. from 1954, later an Oxford don in English
literature, was very clear in conversation that Eric wished to establish himself
on a national stage.[73] Leeson's comments quoted earlier to the Winchester
fellows suggests that Leeson may have encouraged such an ambition. Eric
later confirmed this by describing himself as an 'educational politician'.[74]

By so doing, he accepted that he might enter a wider and more controversial world. Such an ambition affected M.G.S in a particular way. By accepting full participation in the direct grant grammar school scheme just prior to his appointment, the governors put themselves at the apex of the new framework of state secondary education, a talisman for the grammar school selective system as a whole.[75] As such, M.G.S. became a school offering over 500 free places to boys, paid for by Manchester and neighbouring local authorities. Now able to select the most able boys, regardless of the lottery of money or geography, as Eric pithily put it, the school had no need of fee-paying feeder schools.[76] Consequently, almost his first decision on arrival was to recommend the closure of Sale High School, the remaining fee-paying feeder school. There was a row, given that fee-paying parents no longer had a virtual guarantee that their sons could progress without examination to M.G.S. at 11. Why, Eric asked, does M.G.S. need fee-paying preparatory schools now that any boy of real academic ability could be admitted to the school? The governors backed the High Master.[77] Perhaps more questionably, he also withdrew from the Hugh Oldham Lads Club in Ancoats, which had been closely linked to the school since the late nineteenth century and supported by masters and boys. Eric stated he wanted working class boys in his school, not in neighbourhood boys clubs. Interestingly, by the time he left to come to York, he was noting with considerable enthusiasm the work of the school's social services unit within the wider Manchester community.[78]

M.G.S. was newsworthy and not only in the city, given that the Manchester Guardian was at its reputational peak as a national newspaper. Eric and Cordelia quickly engaged in this civic life, in the Manchester Philosophical and Literary Society, as a member of the regional council of the BBC, attending Hallé concerts, with Cordelia becoming a magistrate with an especial interest in juvenile justice. Eric also reviewed widely, accepted speaking engagements and wrote two short books on educational policy and philosophy. He was an energetic man, who quickly graduated into a national role as a member of the Secondary Schools Examination Council, the Central Advisory Council for Education (England), the University Grants Committee, most unusually for a school master at that time, from 1949-58, chairman of the Headmasters' Conference (H.M.C.) in 1953-4. He was knighted in 1956 and made a life peer in the second Macmillan list in 1958.[79]

The range of Eric's activities outside Manchester Grammar School from 1945 until 1960 was enormous – local, regional and national through speeches, book reviews, broadcasting, dinners and membership of educational bodies.[80]

The James Family

White Street Derby

Eric as Deputy Head boy

Eric at Oxford on the river

Eric at Oxford - the young chemist

The half blue at chess - forty years on

The young Alpinist

The young Winchester don

The new High Master Eric 1945

Eric and Cordelia James

As the 1950s progressed the debate over the post war educational settlement began to polarise. Once freed from his responsibilities as Chairman of the HMC, Eric was able to engage more robustly in the emerging argument over selective secondary education. He wrote three long feature articles for the *Sunday Times* in January 1954 on the Crisis in Education. The first is his most articulate defence of the grammar school system in general, the second is about the need for balance in the grammar school curriculum system and the third is on the continuing critical significance of the home background, the importance of extra-curricular activities and his doubts about the rise of commercialism. It is significant that the articles hardly refer to any aspect of education beyond the grammar school. 'It is the abler child from the poor economic and social background that has the scales weighted against him by being denied access to a selective school.'[81]

Later in the year, he addressed the Lancashire and Cheshire heads in the invited presence of Hugh Gaitskell and the Labour Party front bench education team of Michael Stewart and Alice Bacon and to which we have Gaitskell's reaction in his personal diary. Both are quoted fully in appendix 3.[82]

Looking across all this activity, four themes emerge for present purposes. Of the greatest importance was the central place in Eric's thinking of the Direct Grant Grammar School within the new pattern of universal state provision of secondary grammar, technical and modern schools. In 1945 there was wide, if not universal, acceptance that one could rationally and scientifically identify learning types among children at about the age of 11 as between academic, technical and manual. As a consequence, the new universal secondary school system would be founded on this confident assumption, but with variations according to local differences. There was also a naive optimism that there could and would be individual mobility between systems locally if it was seen that the assessment at eleven had not been accurate. Within this structure the 150 or so Direct Grant Grammar Schools, already in existence, provided the apex. Largely situated within significant urban centres and with strong academic traditions, they could provide a ladder of academic opportunity for the most able – free and open to all because public transport enabled children to move easily from home to school. They provided through objective selection, as Eric saw it, the chance for the most talented to obtain the right education without the risk associated with the lottery of money or local geography. Put another way, the Direct Grant Grammar Schools provided a universally free education for very able children, which in a more limited form Eric had secured twenty five years before in Southampton, by luck.[83]

Additionally, these Direct Grant Schools were seen by Eric as firmly within the state's provision, not as independent schools receiving state support. Selective within the grammar school system itself, they would serve a particular social and national purpose in the post-war world. Here we come back to Eric, the scientist with his passionate espousal of the place that science and technology would take in the post-war world and as expressed so urgently in the common room at Winchester in 1940. For him, this new world would be a scientific and technical one, which required much larger numbers of able, highly trained, humane and scientific personnel with qualities of leadership and inspiration to solve the complex problems of modern western society. Such a leadership would be nurtured within the grammar school, and in the direct grant schools in particular, enabling boys and girls to have access to universities freely, well equipped for advanced academic work. They were to be specialist institutions akin to music and art colleges, but nationally distributed and on a much larger scale to cater for the most able. As such, their selectivity would ensure that able children were not to be held back by the less able, and at the same time the schools would offer attractive careers to that limited supply of men and women with a particular talent to inspire and teach able children.[84]

Then there was the question of what should be the weighting within the curriculum of subject specialisation alongside a more wide-ranging general education. Of course, there was no single answer as too many variables were involved as between individual and social need, finance, politics and broadly 'the spirit of the times'. In very general terms, Eric accorded significance to extending science provision at Manchester and a new science block was built and paid for by the founders of Marks and Spencer. Beyond this, he was less sure. Among the most able, he was certain that any future national 'aristocracy of talent', drawn from all subject disciplines, needed both a scientific literacy and a broad humane understanding – a view that he brought fully to the early debates on the curriculum at York. As for the majority of children, he was less confident and probably less informed. They are almost no examples among his speeches and lectures where he addresses specifically the question of whether children educated within the system of Secondary Modern Schools were being equally well served by the post 1944 settlement as it was being implemented across the country. Nor did he highlight that the original intention of the 1944 Act was to establish Secondary Technical Schools as well as County Colleges for education beyond the school leaving age, ambitions that had not been realised except in a few local authorities. By the late 1950s these were becoming urgent issues as was reflected in the enquiries set up in 1956 under Sir Geoffrey Crowther about raising the school leaving age and under Sir John Newsom in 1961 on the needs of the less able child. More locally, it was clear that, irrespective of official policies of the political parties, the debate about a more integrated comprehensive system of secondary education was gaining momentum.[85] This was a weakness on Eric's part. He could state his opinions robustly and did so both publicly and privately. These were positive qualities especially when expressed elegantly and with humour, but they could stimulate strong reactions among those for whom greater overall social equality was more important than simply improving the ladder of opportunity for the academically talented. There was a growing polarisation of opinion on these questions from the late 1950s and it diminished Eric's overall effectiveness as an 'educational politician' thereafter.[86]

Finally, there was the theme of the critical need to encourage, recruit, train and develop the best quality teachers in schools and universities; a topic of engagement for Eric across his whole career from 1945 until 1973. For him, the individual teacher had the greatest impact and influence on the child or young adult, regardless of the social situation or the abilities of the individual student. The best teachers deserved the highest level of public esteem, but it had to be earned and sustained. More particular was his concern expressed through his UGC membership about the critical shortage of high quality teachers in mathematics and science, and how the attractions and remuneration of a research career were sucking away the most talented from teaching and inspiring the future generations of scientists and engineers.[87]

By 1960, Eric had become probably the most renowned headmaster of his day, leading the most successful academic school within the framework established by the 1944 Act, as an exemplar of a particular vision of public education as a ladder of educational opportunity. This system was based on an assumption that a child's qualities and potential could be identified at a reasonably young age. For Eric, the grammar school system and the direct grant schools in particular were the most rational response to the scientific and managerial needs of an increasingly technocratic society. At the same time, the grammar school curriculum and ethos should recognise the humane and civilising traditions of past learning, enabling the pupil's moral and spiritual development to occur alongside the growth of scientific knowledge and its application for human improvement. For some it was a re-invigoration of the ideals of Thomas Arnold, but one which recognised that an explicitly Christian underpinning of selective or elite education was no longer plausible in the mid-twentieth century. But such an education for contemporary society must not become simply vocational or technocratic either, and that the nineteenth century idea of a 'clerisy' - a non-clerical national elite of trained, humane and civilised men and women could be fashioned for the post-war world of science and technology – a 'new aristocracy of talent'. For others, James was seen as the antithesis of a more directly egalitarian model, in which education had a more ambitious role as an interventionist engine of social reconstruction, centred on non-selection, the expansion of schools based on comprehensive principles and with a much greater attention to needs and ambitions of the majority of children. By the time of Eric's appointment to York, this latter model was in the ascendant across a whole spectrum of educational, social and political opinion. This was a change that intensified as the political climate more generally moved against the Conservative government of Harold Macmillan, and towards two decades of more liberal and egalitarian opinion that only came to an end with Mrs Thatcher's election in 1979.[88]

As far as universities were concerned, these shifts of attitude were only indirectly relevant in 1960. Universities were seen as selective in their very nature with the idea of a comprehensive university being a contradiction in terms. For the UGC, the issue was more about responding to the successes of the 1944 Act, rather than its failures, in enabling increasing numbers of highly able and qualified children from a much wider range of backgrounds to progress naturally into a demanding but still highly selective university system. At the same time mandatory student grants for fees and means tested maintenance support became universally available, with the result that universities were to become for the 1960s what the 'Direct Grant' had been for the grammar school in 1945.

The University of York 1960-1973

Within this thinking the local enthusiasts for a university in York had secured a very positive response from the UGC in 1960, and in the person of Eric James they believed they had found the hand to realise their vision. The next twelve years would test whether they were right.

If the members of the University of York's Promotion Committee believed they had secured the right man for the job, what were the blocks already in place on which Eric could build?

He had, firstly, a commitment from the UGC to establish a new university in York and had an experienced and powerful Academic Planning Board to support, guide and ultimately approve the kind of university that was evolving. In its chairman, Lord Robbins, he had an eminent critical friend, a man at the centre of the metropolitan political and cultural establishment, who simultaneously was preparing his report and recommendations for the government on what should be the future size and shape of the university system as a whole. Secondly, he had a locally fashioned vision for a university endorsed by the UGC. He had a physical site at Heslington, the option on some historic buildings in the city, some promises of money from the Rowntree and Morrell charitable trusts and the confectionary firm of Rowntree, and some support from the local authorities. He also had the experience of the York Academic Trust (later the University of York Promotion Committee) and in particular that of John West-Taylor in relation to academic planning and development. What he did not have were any academic or administrative staff, or architects or other professional experts. Personally, he had no previous experience of leadership within universities or in dealing directly with the machinery of central government. He had only tentative support from York City Council.

Consequently, he had to articulate a ten year development plan for the university and secure the plan's endorsement by the UGC. Then he had to appoint and lead a team of architects, planners, administrators and academics so as to admit 200 students by October 1963 into a residential university in an atmosphere of intense public interest and expectation. Along with others, he had simultaneously to devise instruments of governance under a Royal Charter that needed to be both legally robust and sufficiently flexible to adapt as the institution evolved. Informing this essentially practical project, he had also to show that spirit of innovation in the university system that had led Murray and his colleagues to champion the establishment of new universities themselves.

By the time of his retirement in 1973 he had delivered the ten year plan almost totally, leaving an institution of 2000 students, academic and other staff, on a campus that had visually and architecturally secured the positive endorsement of Pevsner, although it also had its critics, and with a public reputation that secured many thousand high quality applicants for its degree courses. This took place within a democratic structure of institutional governance with departments that were autonomous, viable, flourishing and earning national and international reputations in innovation, research and teaching. There had also been exciting additional opportunistic developments along the way, though some parts of the scheme had worked less well than others. This achievement had also been secured in a decade during which the overall political, social, economic and cultural environment had changed dramatically across the globe. At the time of his retirement in 1973, it was not unreasonable for Lord Robbins to say that the University of York was the most successful of all of the British new universities. Characteristically, and still only 64, Eric commented that he should retire believing that he had run out of new ideas.[89]

The discussion of the evolution of the university that follows can only concentrate on a few aspects and on those three elements identified earlier in Eric's educational personality in 1945.

Firstly, 'presence', that most difficult quality to define of transformational leadership; an ability to impress, convince, inspire, at times annoy, something beyond management that makes you want to sign up to the person, work for them, someone who gives you the confidence that there are men and women with qualities beyond the ordinary, beyond your own, somehow exceptional. All those who have written or spoken about Eric James saw him as such a person. Not exactly the same man as in 1945, the fifteen years at Manchester had fashioned him personally and in the public mind. He was now more authoritative, more confident, more controversial, but also less tested as he joined the small group of Vice-Chancellors challenged to establish a new type of university in Britain.[90]

Secondly, there is Eric as the rational, liberal-minded and committed scientist, the man who passionately believed in the positive virtues of science and their application for human betterment in terms of life, work and happiness, and, most notably for him, through the educational system.

Thirdly, there is the same liberal-minded, rational and humane believer in the philosophical, artistic, musical and literary achievements of the human spirit from the past, as the frame within which humans might better themselves at the same time as improving the lives of others.

Having accepted the offer to be the founding Vice-Chancellor, Eric met Archbishop Ramsey on February 14th 1961 and was able to contribute to the draft Interim Report of the Academic Planning Board before it was considered by the UGC on the 9th March. This report reflected the original submissions by the University of York Promotion Committee to the UGC in December 1959, the deliberations prior to the acceptance of York's case, and the work done by the Academic Planning Board since October 1960. The Academic Planning Board had been keen that Eric should have the chance to comment upon the draft prior to its despatch. Eric was always extremely positive about how Robbins handled the Academic Planning Board and that there was nothing in its Interim Report that he wished to challenge in general terms.[91] The two men worked together closely and well and it is important to see Robbins as a significant member of that small group of men who founded and created the character of the University. As in the case of John West-Taylor, Robbins' particular contribution to York is now less well recognised because of his later fame resulting from his widely influential report on student numbers more generally.[92]

Robbins and James saw the new universities in similar ways in relation to contemporary society. They were in a sense a natural culmination of the 1944 Education Act; Eric had always been a straight-forward expansionist during his time as member of the UGC and continued in this vein as Vice-Chancellor. He did not believe 'more meant worse' as many Vice-Chancellors of the time did. He believed that these new institutions should have high academic standards. He supported a relatively small number of traditional academic departmental disciplines, but each of a viable size, a view broadly shared by Robbins. They did not agree so consistently on matters of the curriculum, where Eric was less enamoured of the Scottish system than Robbins.[93] But they did agree that some resolution had to be achieved in reconciling academic depth and breadth, which in York's case involved single subject and main/combined honours degrees, not schools of studies as at East Anglia and Sussex, nor through the general/honours degrees as in Scotland.

The only exception to this pattern at York was in the social sciences. Here it is sufficient to note that the social sciences were the one academic area of university academic development that had already been given quite firm shape prior to Eric's appointment. Two figures were important here. The first, mentioned earlier, is William Wallace, chairman of the Rowntree Company from 1952-7, and in 1959 Chairman of the Joseph Rowntree Memorial Trust, who had since his retirement from Rowntree had become actively involved in the campaign for a university. As the Chairman of the JRMT, he was an important figure, especially in relation to the potential for the development of teaching and research in the social sciences. [94] While the detail is not clear, it seems very likely that both Robbins and Wallace had firm ideas on how social sciences should be structured at York, with primacy given to Economics, with other disciplines – Sociology, Politics, Social Administration – integrated into a single Social Sciences undergraduate degree for the first five terms. Furthermore, it was envisaged that the same disciplines would collaborate in post-graduate teaching and research through an Institute of Social and Economic Research within which Economics would be the dominant disciplinary methodology. Close links would be maintained with the various Rowntree Trusts. Clearly the support of the Rowntree Company and Trusts had been an important element in securing a favourable outcome for York's original bid, but how that relationship might develop seems to have gone further in this area than in any other prior to Eric's appointment.[95] It is therefore perhaps not surprising that the first senior academic appointment should be the Head of the Economics Department, Professor Alan Peacock. As a former pupil of Robbins, Peacock had already been approached by his former tutor about the position, and before he had met Eric himself.[96] Seeds here were unwittingly sown that would cause later difficulties.

Both Robbins and James supported the idea that society needed a new 'aristocracy of talent' for contemporary society and that the new universities were being founded to achieve that ambition through innovative thinking, a dedication to teaching, fundamental research and new institutional practices and structures. They felt that older universities needed waking up and should become more democratic, engaging the non-professorial staff in deliberation, decision making and responsibility. They should not simply be places open from nine until five, but residential institutions providing what we would now describe as the full student experience. In York's case, this involved not having a conventional Senate or Faculties, but a dispersed system of departmental Boards of Studies made up of all the academic staff reporting to a General Academic Board, of whose members only one-third could be Professors, the remainder being elected by the academic staff as a whole. The authority of Professorial Board, on the other hand, was to be limited to issues of promotion and appointments outside their own departments. Not by temperament a 'committee' man, Eric later enthused about such a system as producing some of the best debates on academic matters in his experience, enabling the University of York to be the most democratic of all at the time.[97]

The feature most commented on at the time of the university's founding was that it was to be collegiate, a unique experiment to see if a traditional system built up over many centuries could be re-invented for the twentieth century. It is not clear who first expressed the hope that a university in York should be founded on a collegiate basis. Before the government's decision to establish the new universities, as distinct from the earlier model of 'university colleges', the ambitions of the York Academic Trust had been to establish such a 'university college' in distinctive ways as has been discussed earlier. But once the Trust had rapidly to develop a plan for a fully autonomous university, catering for arts, social science and science with larger numbers of resident students, a wholly different set of critical issues had to be addressed. The collegiate ambition, however, was not included in the briefing notes for the informal meeting with Sir Keith Murray at Bishopthorpe in June 1959, nor does it seem to have been raised in discussion. However, by the time the official submission was made to the UGC in December it was included as an ambition, rather than as a critical element. There is no firm archival evidence or oral testimony to pinpoint those responsible for its inclusion but there can be little doubt that it had become an important part of Milner-White's vision, drawing on his 20 years' experience at King's College, Cambridge and which had been reflected in his earlier ideas of a College for Britain in York., modelled on All Souls' College in Oxford. The UGC were non-committal about the idea, doubting its feasibility, and Michael Ramsey had agreed that, if critical to securing endorsement, the York-based promoters would accept something along the lines of what was planned for Sussex. It made York exceptional from the beginning at least in terms of aspirations and it was a feature likely to irritate civil servants and the Treasury alike.[98] Once the UGC had decided that York's bid should be accepted, Robbins and the newly formed Academic Planning Board did not express an opinion but repeated that the York Promotion committee were very keen. Murray was probably broadly in favour of the idea as part of his vision for a re-invigorated university system and from his own recent experience as Rector of Lincoln College, Oxford. In addition, Lady Ogilvie and Sir William Hodge, as members of the Academic Planning Board, were heads of college in Oxford and Cambridge. The question had not advanced much by the time of Eric's acceptance of the Vice-Chancellorship but he immediately adopted the notion with enthusiasm. He saw its potential in outline as providing a full and comprehensive educational experience for students and their teachers, as well as creating more intimate learning communities in association with the academic departments but within the larger whole. The university at York was to provide an integrated residential, social, cultural and educational experience with teaching, learning and research at the core – Winchester, Henry Morris' Village Colleges and a 'mini-city' all rolled into one.[99]

How all this was to be realised on the ground was the most immediately important task that faced the incoming Vice-Chancellor. Key decisions had to be made almost at once and that meant, first of all, the appointment of architects. Eric later commented that he did not know much about architecture in 1960. Winchester had been there since the middle ages and M.G.S had been largely rebuilt in the early 1930s. Now he had to transform a run-down country house and demesne and some scattered historic buildings in the city and turn them into a university. On the other hand, John West-Taylor did know about architects and his role proved critical. Along with his earlier association with Henry Morris and his role as quasi-director of York's Institute of Architectural Studies, John had a pretty clear idea who he wanted – Robert Matthew Johnson-Marshall (RMJM), a Hertfordshire based partnership, with a strong track record of public sector building, a distinctive way of working with a team of clients, partners and architects, and a practice that had been closely engaged on school building programmes in London. Many of the architects involved had also been strongly influenced by Henry Morris and his Cambridgeshire Village Colleges, most notably Stirrat Johnson-Marshall, whose practice was associated with a vigorous school building programme in Hertfordshire led by John Newsom, the Director of Education, himself almost certainly influenced by Morris. While other partnerships were discussed, it was clear which would be John's preferred choice. Eric agreed, having some knowledge of the practice's work in Hertfordshire, probably through John Newsom and Harry Rée, then Headmaster of Watford Grammar School, a long-standing personal friend, and also a disciple of Morris. All four (Newsom, James, Rée and Morris) will also have known one another through the All Souls Group.[100] Robbins' Academic Planning Board agreed and so the partnership nominated a young architect, Andrew Derbyshire, to take the lead in the first instance and to formulate the Development Plan. At roughly the same time, a new director was appointed to the Institute of Advanced Architectural Studies, Patrick Nuttgens, and he became the fourth member of the quartet, which set about building a university.[101]

One of the many reasons for the quartet so enjoying the task was Eric's style of working. Clearly not the expert, he was nevertheless in charge and relished the intellectual, technical, logistical, financial and political challenges of such a huge and innovative project. The choice of RMJM was inspired, as their innovative method of working chimed with all the individual temperaments involved. For architects, largely in the public sector, they were unusually client-focussed, engaging Eric and John in highly detailed enquiry, something Eric later called 'continuous inquisition' as to what kind of university they wanted. Full day meetings were held monthly over a ten year period and were of a 'dialectical' character. What this meant was that Eric had almost immediately to answer detailed academic as well as architectural questions for which he had no prepared answer and no academic colleagues to consult or confer with. As the focus of the campus was to be collegiate in ways not yet discussed, there were inter-connected educational, domestic, architectural and building issues concerning residence, catering, social and public space, and how each was to be integrated within a complex of linked buildings that also had to provide for teaching and research in the humanities and social sciences. There were to be no faculty buildings other than laboratories. Were departmental academic staff, for instance, to be located within a single college or were they to be dispersed? What was the teaching method to be across the range of disciplines and how would that impact on the pattern of offices, seminar rooms, libraries and lecture halls? These and many other discussions flowed together during conversations in York and Manchester, often in the Yorkshire Club, next to Lendal Bridge. But there were also more immediately pressing issues to be addressed. How were the historic buildings to be brought back into use quickly, how was additional land to be secured and who was to pay for it, how were the colleges to be funded, as the UGC would not pay for any of the residential accommodation or social space before the first students arrived?[102]

Two framing decisions turned out to be fundamental. Both related to the condition of the site which was poorly drained and not able to support high-rise buildings in quantity. The first was resolved by deciding to construct an artificial lake as the functional environment around which to situate the university buildings. The second was to build using a pre-fabricated system called CLASP rather than the more conventional bricks and mortar.[103] Both remained fundamental to the university as it developed over the next thirty years, and has formed an important element in planning the landscape on the second campus on Heslington East over the last fifteen years. Each decision was technically complex and generated considerable debate at the time and subsequently. The idea of the lake was probably Stirrat Johnson-Marshall's and would have been quickly endorsed by John West-Taylor as an imaginative solution to a technical problem of land drainage. The second, the use of the CLASP system of prefabricated building still continues to divide both architects and the university community. Many have claimed that it was adopted simply on grounds of cost, but there is no substantive evidence that this was the determining element. Most important for Eric, illustrative of his leadership style, was emphatically to drive the team to find answers so that the project was delivered on time and on budget, as it was. Speed of construction, light weightings, inherent flexibility, and a shortage of labour and bricks all contributed to the decision. For Eric it was absolute essential that the fledgling university be ready for its first students in October 1963. Following on from these two key decisions, the whole ten year programme for the campus could be mapped in outline around the lake and on the north of University Road. Within this frame, the colleges were core elements situated within the overall vision of an integrated built environment, connected by walkways to the stand-alone buildings – the library, the laboratories and the central hall and with pleasant and varied vistas. All of this was to be achieved progressively over the ten year period without the university being a permanent building site. Eric found himself in these debates as an architectural modernist, perhaps to his surprise. Not all were quite so sure, with some of the city fathers looking for more ivy and Gothicism, or a 'cut-down Keble' as Eric expressed it. The overall result will continue to be a matter of opinion, but most regard it as a success. There are few landmark buildings, the uncontrolled costs of Sir Basil Spence's scheme at Sussex guaranteed that the UGC would not allow that mistake again. Denys Lasdun's scheme at East Anglia looks more exciting in part, but, as John West-Taylor later asked, 'would you want to live in some of those buildings?'. The landscaping was inspired, so that the ever nostalgic Dean Milner-White could be reminded of the Backs. Pat Nuttgens preferred to see it as 'a humane and non-pompous place'.[104]

Of course, policy decisions, particularly those of relating to the academic development of the University, became increasingly more than four men talking about the site in the Yorkshire Club, as the key academic appointments were made of the founding departmental heads along with the librarian. Appointing inspiring staff is probably the most important responsibility of any headmaster and Eric had that talent and experience, all of which he brought to York. It was, probably, his single most significant personal contribution to the founding of the university. Moreover, on paper at least he did not have a free hand, as all founding senior staff had to be approved by Robbins and the Academic Planning Board. There was also the question of who would be attracted by the risk in accepting such posts in a totally untested institution. By Eric's own account, the Board only cavilled once about a recommendation, and 'they were right'. This almost certainly refers to the headship of the History Department and Eric's initial recommendation of the Oxford historian, Lawrence Stone. His general method in making the founding academic appointments would now be regarded as very bad practice – no role descriptions, no person specification, no advertisement, no presentations or appointments committee – just interviews with Eric, often at the Athenaeum. Looking across the eight or so founding heads – Peacock, Brockbank, Moodie, Aylmer, Norman, Williamson, Heavens, Kennedy and others – we see a group of diversely talented men that Eric could engage with, while also allowing them to fashion their own departments in ways that they believed were innovative and imaginative. He would also listen to them and was ultimately pragmatic in the face of differences of view. He had to give way to Robbins'and Peacock's insistence that economics should have its own focussed fiefdom in Alcuin, he accepted Peacock's and Brockbank's arguments that single-sex colleges would simply create more trouble than they were worth.[105]

Although Eric was not seen at the time as so much of an innovator as some other new university Vice-Chancellors in respect of new academic disciplines or degree structures, he nevertheless engaged closely with the questions of how a particular discipline should be established and taught at York. He endorsed the idea that English and foreign literatures should be taught in a single department and that Language (including English, European and non-European languages) and Linguistics should be also taught comparatively within an autonomous separate single department. Both were innovative developments with practical benefits of scale, avoiding the creation of micro-departments focussed on a single language and its literature.[106] He also supported both heads of English and History in their commitment to mediaeval studies (an element not found in any other of the 'new universities'). In Politics, he was sensitive to earlier ideas of the King's Manor being the site of a staff college for local government and so public administration and government was one of the key elements in that department's formation. In Biology, he supported the idea of an integrated undergraduate degree in the subject rather than repeating the pattern of separate degrees in botany, zoology etc. He regretted the refusal of the UGC to sanction a school of architecture, despite the university's prior experience through the Institute of Advanced Architectural Studies.[107]

But as well as implementing the original academic plan agreed with the UGC, Eric was also imaginatively opportunistic. Once someone impressed him as having potential, then he set about overcoming routine difficulties. 'Why not?' was one of his familiar responses to a new idea. In the case of his own subject, Chemistry, he quickly established that Richard Norman was the man he wanted. But Dick was first of all a research chemist, not very interested in bricks, mortar and committees. Eric's response was typical; he found a young chemist teaching at Wellington College, David Waddington, made him a senior lecturer with the responsibility for establishing the first laboratories in the university and got what he wanted. It also started a commitment within the department to exploring the relationships between Chemistry and Education, something very close to Eric's own thinking. He did much the same with Biology. Mark Williamson was not able to take up his appointment immediately, so a young biologist, John Currie, was appointed to take the project forward. Nothing could be further from the present practice of starting with the appointment of a spectacularly expensive professorial 'star' as a founding head, and then wondering why the person turns out to be more of a prima donna than a star. [108] Two further examples are relevant. There had been no intention to establish a Music department immediately at York, but it was part of Eric's ambition for the university to a have a distinctive arts presence on the campus. Through his Manchester-based friendship with Sidney Bernstein, a Granada arts fund was established which supported a visiting fellowship in music, the first holder of which was the young David Blake. It was such a success that Eric was persuaded that music should feature prominently within the academic disciplines at York. Never attracted simply by a 'safe pair of hands', Eric appointed Wilfrid Mellers, with the result that one of the most innovative and imaginative Music departments in the country came into being. It also established a link with F.R.Leavis, Mellers' tutor and friend in Cambridge, who later became a visiting Professor in the English department. The same happened in the History of Art just before Eric retired. In some way, the figure of Richard Verdi came across his bows – again possibly through Manchester connections – an inspirational and charismatic young art historian. He was appointed as a lecturer jointly in the departments of History and English, out of which eventually the History of Art Department was born. The development of stained glass studies, capitalising on the unique inheritance of the city of York, came about in much the same way, supported by the Mellon Foundation. It is interesting that these developments were all in the field of the practising arts, subjects not close to the thinking of the Treasury or the UGC, but very close to Eric's philosophy of creating a campus on which students and staff in all disciplines were surrounded by humane learning, practice and performance.[109]

Education was not a leading feature in the original plan either. Not unexpectedly, Eric had vigorous views about education as an academic discipline, but he could see that there would be students, who were already set on a teaching career at the age of eighteen and wanted an academic training as well as practical guidance on schools and teaching. He was also committed to encouraging as many of the most able academically to consider teaching as a profession. The pattern of teacher training in England in the 1960s was chaotic and unsystematic as a result of the historic evolution of training for the profession. Consequently, it was decided that York should try to make a constructive contribution through the combined degree structure, with an academic subject as the main focus but with education in combination. In addition, there was the problem of students in all disciplines being unable to master foreign languages. The two were brought together in two appointments – again both adventurous – of Harry Rée, headmaster of Watford Grammar School, as head of the Education department and Eric Hawkins, also a headmaster, as director of the Language Teaching Centre. Again it is worth noting how Eric did not accept that prior experience in schools was in any way a disadvantage in seeking the best person to appoint in universities, nor did he believe that university academics were not fitted to take senior posts within schools.[110]

Not all of the founding academic decisions and appointments were a success. One of the original heads of department did not last long and another tragically took his own life. But probably the most challenging element in these early appointments and academic decisions was in the social sciences. Here we return to Lord Robbins. We saw earlier that the York Academic Trust, and William Wallace in particular, had been especially keen to secure Robbins as the chairman of the York Academic Planning Board. Once appointed, Robbins remained a significant influence on the evolution of the Economics department and its early appointees including the founding head, Professor Alan Peacock and Jack Wiseman, the first head of the Institute of Social and Economic Research. Others early members of the department, Douglas Dosser and Ron Cooper, were already known to either Robbins or Peacock.[111]

The second area in which Robbins certainly had some role was in the form of the undergraduate degree. Economics was in many respects the original social science with its founding home in late eighteenth century Edinburgh, and with its claims to seniority not always being confined to the historical record. Robbins shared some of this hauteur. He did not support, for instance, the idea of Sociology as suitable as an undergraduate subject and had to be assured by Eric that its teaching at York would be strictly 'empirical'. Whether connected or not, Peacock and his early colleagues wished that the social sciences should be taught atypically at York through an integrated part I structure, in which the student took compulsory courses for the first two years before being able to specialise – rather like the LSE or the Scottish model. Eric's general view as expressed earlier was not in favour of 'schools' of studies, which is what this was essentially, but had to compromise. It was not a success. The students disliked its dirigisme, academic staff in the other departments such as Politics and Sociology felt constrained. Coincidentally, these disciplines themselves were also developing in different directions in the slightly torrid intellectual environment of the late 1960s. For all sorts of reasons, the LSE was not always the example you wished to follow at that time. In his valedictory interview in 1973 Eric predicted that it would have to break up, which it did quite soon after his retirement.[112]

The third area of Robbins' influence was more successful, but not quite in the way originally intended. As we have seen Robbins was also involved in the work of the Rowntree Trusts by his membership of the Social Services Trust and through his discussions with William Wallace. The support of the Rowntree Trusts had been an important element in the case made to the UGC in December 1959. That support was not just financial, it also had an academic dimension, given the research aspect to the Trusts' work in the social sciences, both pure and applied. These interests preceded the decision to establish the University, usually being through ideas for further institutes in social research and policy. With a real prospect of achieving a full university in 1960 these ideas came forward again vigorously and were focussed on the idea of an Institute of Economic and Social Research, which under Jack Wiseman's directorship would be the co-ordinating umbrella for a whole school of institutes and centres. Once again, the conception turned out to be too dirigiste and too dominated by those who were economists. Most notably, the redoubtable head of the newly established Department for Social Administration and Social Work, Kathleen Jones, was not going to be constrained in this way. Ultimately the university had to accept a greater degree of autonomy among these centres. But the engagement with the range of social services, the research underpinning their provision along with a 'campaigning' dimension has remained a distinctive and distinguished part of the university's development, both domestically and in association with the Rowntree Trusts.

The fourth aspect of Eric's Vice-Chancellorship relates to how he treated the students themselves and how he was regarded. This is not easy to pin down as any evidence is likely to be contradictory, much of it being as much about impressions as deeds, both at the time and in retrospect. There is the testimony of those students of the time, who came into contact with him directly and would tend to be those acting as student representatives or student journalists. There would also be those who faced him in his disciplinary capacity. Evidence from such sources often changes as students' own lives develop. A good example is Tony Banks (later a Labour life peer), a firebrand at York who mellowed later.[113] Others, not many, found his head-masterliness patronising, not a wholly unusual reaction from insecure but able young men in the 1960s.[114] And that makes another point. Totally unexpectedly, universities and schools were faced with an apparent sea change in student attitudes – at least among a significant minority – to traditional forms of authority, to conventional politics, institutionally, locally and nationally, and in their personal behaviour. Some British universities were seriously disrupted for a period – the LSE, Warwick and Essex most notably, and that was but a shadow of what erupted in Paris and on some US campuses. So it is not easy to make an assessment of how Eric handled these changes at York.[115]

For whatever reason, York was not seriously disrupted during these years – there was one strike about the catering in 1968 and one sit-in in 1970, in sympathy with the students at Warwick, over a dispute with their university about whether secret personal files were held on them. Both were essentially domestic disputes, but made more dramatic because of the general atmosphere of student activism. Ironically, there were more significant domestic confrontations between the university and its students under Eric's less paternal successor, Maurice Carstairs, with sit-ins becoming almost an annual fixture in the mid-1970s. The largest student demonstration, in fact, occurred just 18 months before Eric's retirement, which was a public protest and a march through the streets of York in response to the events in Londonderry on Bloody Sunday on January 30th 1972, when British troops fired upon civilians at the beginning of the Troubles in Northern Ireland. This protest involved both staff and students, with Gerald Aylmer, the head of the History department, walking alongside the marchers in order to observe whether the police behaved appropriately and legally. On campus, a mass debate and teach-in was held in the largest lecture theatre, involving both staff and students on the situation in Northern Ireland and how it should be understood economically, politically and historically.[116]

So in a complex web of evidence, two very different perspectives on Eric's reactions to the changes in student attitudes and behaviour in the late 1960s will be outlined. The first is to ask how he saw the phenomenon of political activism and changing student behaviour more generally, which was a subject of two serious debates in the House of Lords and in which Eric spoke. Three strands form the rope of his analysis. The first was a vigorous endorsement of student activism against injustice and illegitimate violence – support for civil rights, hostility to apartheid and doubts about the morality of the Vietnam War. One senses this was familiar ground for a man who had been surrounded by the debates over fascism and the Spanish Civil War at Winchester in the 1930s with its transforming effect on some of those young men's lives. The second was a respect for the demand for greater student participation in the university's governing affairs, especially in respect to those aspects that directly affected the lives of students themselves. In this area he accepted that students had a legitimate case to put and in response to the catering strike by York students in 1968 he asked Graeme Moodie, head of the Politics department, to research the issue and produce a report, which became the defining document on student representation in both social and most academic matters for the next two decades. Eric often wondered aloud why a minority of students wanted to spend time on domestic committees, when there were more interesting things to do when you were 20, but he respected their view and that universities should be places that debated these matters in a rational and civilised way. The third was more personal and moving. Eric was a Reithian. All his life he had gradually been introduced to elements of western culture of quality and value, first from his father's love of literature, then through his own growing interest in painting and music towards the end of his time in Oxford, something on which he was able to capitalise at Winchester, and most recently through his engagement with architects and social planners in setting up the University. For holidays he and Cordelia went walking in the Alps and he became a knowledgeable amateur alpine botanist. He saw schools and public institutions as having ambitions in raising citizens' understanding and enjoyment of elements of human achievement, which they may not have had the good fortune to have acquired within their family environment. Unsurprisingly, he had opposed the introduction of commercial television, seeing it as diluting the educative role of the BBC, graphically commenting that the best time of the day to enhance a child's learning from television, the early evening, was now dominated by Laramie and the Lone Ranger. With this mind set, he found the more uncouth aspects of some students' behaviour, their anti-intellectualism and crude political stereotyping, and on occasion their vandalism, hard to stomach. He put this very personally in his speech. For his generation, the opportunity to go to university had been the greatest privilege and piece of good luck, and he found it hard to accommodate the minority of students who cavalierly disregarded their own good fortune. It was a very finely balanced statement from the man, who had also acquired a student nick-name at York, not the Chief as at M.G.S., but as Lord Jim, which perhaps does something to explain York's relative calm during these years.[117]

The second aspect on how Eric treated students is in relation to how he dealt with individual students. Inevitably over a ten year period, some students had to be disciplined or excluded and it is interesting to see how Eric handled such cases from the surviving documentation, bearing in mind that the age of majority was only raised to 21 in England and Wales in 1969. In each case, Eric had dealt with the individual student personally before a final decision, whether the misdemeanour related to poor performance, drugs, indiscipline, anti-semitism or vandalism. If the student was required to leave, he wrote to the parents in an encouraging way, giving his positive impression of their son or daughter, whose main fault in almost all cases in his opinion had been immaturity, and that he was confident that the incident would not impair their future success and happiness. In one case, in which the student had racially abused a Jewish student, which led to his immediate expulsion, Eric wrote a positive reference for him to work for a local authority to acquire that greater personal maturity. Cordelia acted in the same way, supporting a female student, who had unexpectedly become pregnant, by making baby clothes, or by entertaining younger staff and their children to bonfire night parties in the Vice-Chancellor's garden. When a quite large number of students were arrested in York on the march in protest against the shootings on Bloody Sunday, the Students' Union engaged a young solicitor to defend them before the magistrates. Besides the local journalists, there was a single mature lady in court watching the proceedings, who later wrote to him, thanking him for his defence of the students. It was Cordelia, Lady James, herself a magistrate.[118]

Conclusion

As he came to retire in the autumn of 1973, Eric gave two video interviews with Stuart Sutcliffe in which he reflected on the founding of the University of York and his role as the first Vice-Chancellor. He had already written and spoken about the process and was to do so again with Andrew Saint and James Wilson. There are very few inconsistencies between the accounts, only occasional differences of emphasis. There are also few disagreements with the accounts of the others most closely involved in the construction of the campus and the founding of academic departments and institutes. Nor is the tone in 1973 in any way triumphalist, even though many thought the University of York the most successful of the new universities. Two aspects of the development were seen as not fully proven. On the College system, he commented that the 'jury was still out' on its realising the hopes of the founders, including himself. Secondly, he saw the attempt to create an integrated school of social sciences as having proved much more problematic than anyone had envisaged. He predicted that the social science structure would be broken up.

In writing and speaking so fully throughout his whole career, including the period at York, it is interesting that Eric never seems to have contemplated writing memoirs. Nor in fact did he speak much at all about himself, his background, education and early career. His conversation was about the issues facing him and whosoever was listening. To some degree, this account of Eric's life and career in education has aimed at filling in some of those gaps in knowledge by placing it in the context of England's educational system from the early 1920s until the late 1970s. As far as the University of York is concerned, it has tried to show what sort of educationalist the University of York Promotion Committee has appointed with 'enthusiasm' in early 1961 and incorporating the vision of a University in York they had already developed in collaboration with the UGC. The bringing together of the man and the vision was the achievement of the years from 1961 until his retirement twelve years later; in his words a 'dialectical' association which almost all found exhilarating, inspiring and enjoyable. How then can one summarise Eric's individual contribution to the founding of a new sort of university in York in the later twentieth century?

First, and the most difficult to analyse, is that 'presence' noted by Jeremy Morse as a schoolboy at Winchester during the war and by his Headmaster, Spencer Leeson. It had found expression in the universal title of 'the Chief' at Manchester, and by the student nickname of 'Lord Jim' at York. It is a personal quality easier to experience than describe. But there are clearly individuals who have an exceptional impact on those they meet – Churchill, Mrs Thatcher, Bill Clinton, Mother Theresa and Cardinal Basil Hume are examples frequently quoted in this regard. It is not an unqualifiedly positive quality and, without other attributes, it can simply be seen as 'larger than life', but it is something that Eric possessed and used creatively in his chosen field of English education from his early days at Winchester.

Secondly, Eric was a very able man of diverse talents and potential. Despite his own self-deprecating later comments, he was clearly a very good chemist, who with a different background and at another time might well have moved wholly in the world of science and technology. As it was he used his ability to promote the critical place of science in education at Winchester and Manchester Grammar School along with the Direct Grant system more widely. But this scientific ability and cast of mind also allowed him quickly to master complex technical, administrative, scholarly and academic matters as he demonstrated in the field of architecture and building at York. At the same time he was able to accept new ways of thinking about teaching and research within academic disciplines. He also had the ability, vision and self-confidence to appoint able staff, inspired to work for him enthusiastically, and without the need for micro-management on his part. Such a hands-off approach meant not always winning the argument and a preparedness to work with the majority view. This was the case in the decision to have co-educational colleges and to allow the Economics department to be co-located with sciences in Alcuin College as though it was an empirical science.

Thirdly, Eric did have a coherent vision for academic education in England within both schools and universities. He was a man of the 1944 Education Act and of the decade of informed debate that had preceded it. For him the Act was the defining educational moment for Britain, once the war had been won; a world in which science and technology would be critical for national survival and in creating the 'New Jerusalem' of his Winchester talk in 1940. Academic talents in children had to be sought out and nurtured irrespective of the local social geography or the ability to pay. Those talents needed to be found within science and the arts, each able to inform the child/student's development and education. Academically able staff needed to be recruited to a career that would utilise fully their abilities and ambitions. Selection was inevitable, but it should be on the most open basis possible. In this world the Direct Grant Grammar School, in particular, had a unique part to play. Ladders of opportunity were needed if a 'true aristocracy of talent' was to be encouraged.

Never uncontested as a vision after 1945, it became less convincing from the later 1950s as public opinion generally moved in a more egalitarian direction and as the 1944 Education Act was only implemented in part. For Eric, the core arguments about the need to support academic talent remained the same even as the ways to achieve it became more divisive.

These differences were finely expressed by Eric and his long-standing friend, Baroness Wootton of Abinger, in a House of Lords debate on the Labour party's education policy in 1963.[119] It was probably fortuitous that he left the school system in 1961 and moved to York. Universities were selective by definition in 1960. Paradoxically, one of unintended consequences of the 1944 Education Act was the need 15 years later to found new, innovative and different universities to satisfy the demand from the most able and fortunate beneficiaries of the grammar school system. Access to universities, like the Direct Grant Grammar Schools, should be open to ability, without regard to the lottery of geography or money.

Finally, despite eminence, authority and distinction, Eric retained throughout his life a personal humanity, wisdom and humour that was prepared to devote interest and time to the individual student or staff member as in the examples quoted earlier and in the author's own experience. There are many examples in both Eric and Cordelia's case, but it is sufficient to conclude by recording Eric's parting words to Roger Young as he left Manchester Grammar School to become a headmaster himself, 'A friend for life, Roger.'[120]

Campus construction

An aerial view of the campus

The University's Central Hall

Derwent and Langwith Colleges

The J.B. Morrell Library c. 1969

Stirrat Johnson-Marshall and Andrew Derbyshire

Patrick Nuttgens

Reflections

Eric James retired over 40 years ago and he died more than 20 years ago. The University of which he was founding Vice-Chancellor has just celebrated its 50th anniversary in an educational world very different from that of the quarter century following the Second World War. Nevertheless, it is worthwhile to contemplate what he would think of the University today and its place in what is now called higher education. These can only be personal reflections, but they do come from an author, who has been living closely alongside Eric in researching his career and achievements, and who also worked for over 40 years in the University he created. It would be surprising if there was universal agreement on what follows.

Firstly, he would be proud of the University's continuing success in the now global world of higher education. While deprecating league tables as they applied to schools in the 1950s, he believed in success. He would be especially pleased at the very high quality of the students, their energy and achievements during and after their time at York, and would welcome the diversity of backgrounds from which they come and the variety of their later careers. He believed that the phrase 'an aristocracy of talent' meant something positive.

Secondly, and this may surprise some readers, he would be content with the size of the university. At the time, he was in favour of York remaining small, but more generally he was always an expansionist in terms of overall student numbers, if well qualified applicants sought admission. He would not be one of those present day pundits who say that the system is too large. The planning decision in the early 1960s to assign the land to the east of Heslington church as a possible area for future university growth is a living proof of this.

Thirdly, he would be delighted with some of the new disciplines that are now part of the core teaching and research of the university – History of Art, Medicine, and Law for example. He would continue to regret that York was not able to secure the UGC's approval for a school of Architecture or ultimately sustain the work of the Institute of Advanced Architectural Studies, whose closure he might well regard as short-sighted. It would be quite likely that he would be sceptical about the general growth in Management schools and given his views on commercial broadcasting might be wary about Theatre, Film and TV.

Fourthly he would be dismissive of much of present day ways of assessing academic research as confusing quantity and financial accountability with quality, but he would welcome the more recent emphasis on engagement and impact and the increasing significance of universities in improving the learning, living and working environment of the country. He would be enthusiastic about the Festival of Ideas, student volunteering, and the University's engagement in social justice, human rights and global understanding. In particular, he would have recognised, if sadly, that the problems associated with attracting able and inspirational school teachers in mathematics and science were still national in scale, just as he had reported to his governors in 1946. He would have seen the need for the Centre for Science Education and have welcomed its presence in the University of York.

Fifthly, he would have welcomed the fact that the college system had become embedded within the University's corporate identity. In 1973, he had commented that the 'jury was still out' on the college system and it has evolved in different ways from those he had hoped for, especially as it engages the academic staff across the campus. The ideal of a community of scholars was probably never realisable in a rapidly changing world of marriage, family life, career progression and greater concern for equality more generally; changes which are as true for collegiate universities with centuries of tradition as well as with those trying to create them.

But he would have welcomed the determination to maintain that collegiate structure in relation to students and for undergraduates in particular. In 1960 the UGC was not particularly enthusiastic that York wished to be collegiate, and ever since academic departments and support services centrally in the University have found it less convenient for their operations. Perhaps rather surprisingly, Professor Brian Cantor, on becoming Vice-Chancellor in 2002, declared that the college system was not negotiable and additional colleges are being established on the new campus. Forty years after Eric's retirement and 50 after the opening of Derwent and Langwith, the evidence of the staying power of the collegiate ideal is showing through in terms of what it offers current students in terms of wider experiences and opportunity, in the loyalty and enthusiasm of the alumni, and as an important and distinguishing element in the University's corporate identity.

There are, conversely, several developments that Eric would have found distressing. Firstly, he would be sceptical about the growth in the priority given to individual academic research as encouraging too much research of middling quality. He would regard it as distracting academic staff from their primary role as inspiring teachers of able students in equipping them to make a significant contribution in their chosen careers. Very respectful of research that was truly 'top flight', he would find some of the language used by academic researchers pompous and self-important.

Secondly, he would loathe the current emphasis on corporate management of the university system. As a headmaster and vice-chancellor, he saw enthusiasm, vision, and engagement as the key elements in the leadership of any organisation; management 'wisdom' and pre-occupations with 'process' would receive short shrift. As a man who had to sell a Lowry picture presented to him on his departure from M.G.S. to pay for his home in retirement, he would regard the general level of vice-chancellors' pay as offensive or, if being ironic, surprising.

Thirdly, he would regret the lesser priority given to undergraduate teaching, probably be sceptical of the multiplication of taught graduate programmes, but regard the Student Satisfaction Survey and the concept of the 'Student Experience' as useful antidotes.

Fourthly, he would dislike the increasing levels of centralised control within individual universities and the consequent diminishing of departmental autonomy and the responsibility of the head of department to run and develop the department in their own fashion. He would also think the abolition of the General Academic Board as mistaken in that it removed one of the most significant radical objectives in founding new universities – that of creating greater opportunities for younger academic staff to play a creative part in the development of the university as a whole.

Finally, he would deeply regret the 'functionality' that informed the redevelopment of the north side of the campus in the 1990s and the poorly reflected abandoning of the principles underlying the original development plan. It was a view widely shared and expressed at the time. On the other hand, ironically, the move to develop the new campus in the following decade was so controversial in terms of the public planning process that all the original broad criteria relating to landscaping, human movement, style and arrangement of the buildings and the associated human activity, had to be thought about seriously and professionally, which probably helps to explain its success in progress.

In June 1973 Lord Clark of Saltwood, Chancellor of the University, began his tribute to Eric James, who was about to retire, in the following words:

> The first perfect unit of the Renaissance was the city of Urbino. It was small, compact, yet spacious and luminous. Its inhabitants were content. The city was virtually the creation of one man – Federigo

[da] Montelfeltro, Duke of Urbino. He was a wise and just ruler, a patron of the arts and a great lover of books. And one day his librarian asked him what it was, what it took, to be a good ruler, to which the Duke replied 'essere umano' [to be human].

Well, I didn't explain why I told this tale today. Our Vice-Chancellor has been a wise and just ruler. He has studied the art of education as Federigo studied the art of war, applying a trained intelligence to a complex subject and never losing sight of the ultimate objective... He has been a great patron of the arts, especially art and music, but all these achievements have been given a special lustre, a golden light, by the warmth and humanity of his character.'[121]

Appendix 1: Eric James and Religion

There was much comment during his lifetime and since about Eric James being an atheist and he made it clear that he did not subscribe to a belief in the doctrines of Christianity or practice any faith. This was despite, or perhaps because of, the firm Congregationalist background of his parents. No provision was made at the founding of the University of York for worship by any faith or denomination and the University chaplaincies were independent initiatives by the Church of England (in association with the parish of Heslington) or by the Diocese of Leeds in respect of a Roman Catholic chaplaincy, also in Heslington. For most of the first fifty years of the University, the only provision on the campus was that of an office, from which the chaplains could exercise their pastoral role with student body.

On the other hand, Eric James attended chapel as an assistant master at Winchester, and in his supervision of boys as a 'Div Don' frequently lectured on religious and philosophical topics, usually on historical themes arising from the Judeao-Christian tradition (see Gerald Aylmer's obituary comments on James's lessons on the Minor Prophets) or on Plato and his influence on western thought and culture. At Manchester Grammar School, Eric taught Divinity to the sixth form (see Alan Garner's tribute). It is also true that Eric did not write or speak very often on explicitly Christian themes or to Christian organisations. But he did have a considerable interest in the relationship between the scientific, material world and that of the spiritual and moral universe.

In an essay of this kind, it is not possible to examine those aspects of Eric's intellectual personality in any detail. What follows are two verbatim personal statements by Eric on these questions. They are very different in purpose, one with another. The first is the earliest surviving text of any public address given by Eric to his schoolmasterly colleagues at Winchester in 1940. The second is a copy of a personal letter, quoted by kind permission, from Eric to his sister in law on the premature death of her son in 1951. It focusses in tragic circumstances on whether a belief in the afterlife is sustainable. For a person who did not believe in the literal possibility of life after death, it is a sensitive and thoughtful letter of condolence. Taken together, the two pieces are an interesting commentary on Eric himself, as well as how a thoughtful, intelligent and sensitive man in the mid twentieth century approached these fundamental questions.

Education and Scientific Humanism

16 March 1940[122]

I have three apologies to make for this essay. In the first place I think it is too long. In the second it does not altogether discharge my instructions for it makes no pretence to describe actual technical possibilities but only educational ideas. I decided that to give any idea of the precise nature of scientific advance would demand too much preliminary work on background. Thirdly the essay was written on a cheap line of paper bought at Warren's sale and called for some reason 'sermon paper'. This name seems to have affected my style and I find to my horror on rereading that what I had intended to be the fumbling suggestions of a young and inexperienced teacher read like the assertive <fulminations> pugnacity of a very minor prophet. I hope that you will forgive the humourless dogmatism and prophetic pomposity. The paper is to blame.

This is a very difficult paper to write for several reasons. There will be some here who have heard me preach the same familiar gospel on previous occasions or will have read some of it better done in Hogben or Bernal.[123] There are others who with the best will in the world cannot see what I am getting at. It will appear to them that I am merely saying that with more science in the school time-table and more modern conveniences in home and factory a brave new world will be at hand. They will feel that such a new world is not their choice and that I do not touch the root questions of education at all. And I must admit that what I shall say will be nebulous in its practical content. I cannot say 'teach these subjects and teach them like this and our education will be transformed'. All that I can do is to give some account of the educational implications of the new scientific knowledge. That knowledge is not only relevant of course to public schools, but to the whole field of education, but what I shall say is concerned mainly with the public schools for it is I believe particularly important that such schools should face the problems involved because of their still immensely great educational and social influence.

Firstly, then, let us examine the present situation in the light of what Francis said in his paper.[124] Though I do not rate [Thomas] Arnold as high as Francis [Hill] does as a social force nevertheless I should agree that he was able to infuse new life into the public school because he infused a new idealism, and that idealism was adapted to action in the contemporary society. It was based on Christianity and classical culture, but although it thus had its roots in the past and in the glorification of two slave states, yet it sought to render contemporary life more tolerable by an individual application of the ideals of personal value which Christianity and Greek thought put forward. It was successful because it was practical in a time of expanding liberal capitalism. Much needed to be done; much could be done: much was done. A good deal of the reformist activity of the 19th century was carried out by disinterested and idealistic public school men from whom the new civil service and the new social movements recruited themselves. But we are now all conscious of the slowing down of the process. The symptoms are familiar: a lack, not of good will, but of direction and initiative at the top of our schools and in the universities, a general feeling of frustration: a failure of creative enthusiasm; a movement towards communism as providing the only scope for vision and for action. All these signs we should agree are visible among the boys. Among ourselves we are conscious of unbridgeable gulfs between our various ideals; an over insistence on routine; a false valuation of games. Among both masters and boys there is a general inability to see the relevance of what we teach for the world. We have simply lost faith, and the specious arguments we provide for teaching what we do are evidence of our loss. Recall the meeting on the position of Greek last term. Arnold did not say that he taught Greek as a training for the mind, or to cultivate the memory, or to teach the boys to write English or any nonsense of that sort. Nor did he insist upon chapel because the house from the hours of 5 to 6 is very difficult for housemasters to fill otherwise. He taught Greek and believed in public school Christianity because he thought that an outlook based on Christianity and the classics would provide a steady flame of idealism that would make the boys grow up into men who would create a better world. That vision fails now, and to some extent failed then for two connected reasons. In the first place liberal capitalism cannot go on expanding indefinitely. Orthodox Marxism you will say. Perhaps, but have its implications for the public school boy been sufficiently realised? The self-sacrificing benevolence of a Kingsley or a Hughes becomes today the purely palliative activity of the boys club, that does not attract many of the best. The public school boy of Arnold's day saw an enormous number of ways in which the lot of the working class could be bettered, and he went to better it. The public school boy of today is to a great extent unconsciously bewildered by the fact that we cannot improve working class conditions on those lines much-more because 'someone has to do the dirty work'. Because lower class life was so incredibly bad in Arnold's day and Income tax non-existent, there was room for immediate improvement without worrying about the final inescapable fact that a coal-steel economy inevitably condemns a majority of citizens to live dangerous, filthy and perpetually sordid lives. Now we are face to face with that fact. As the Wykehamist said to me when confronted with the drab grey desert of the Isle of Dogs, 'well I suppose someone has to live here'. There is in fact a limit imposed on our reformism by the apparent technical resources of society and by its structure, and when that limit has been realised reformist idealism has retreated baffled. It is significant that the real Utopia builders of the 19th century, for instance William Morris, looked further into the future than the movements of social benevolence, saw no way out of the dilemma of industrial capitalism except the wrecking of machines and the performance of craft – which though idyllic is really no way out at all. I believe that here we have the first cause of our frustration and our lack of social initiative, and it is because Communism does provide a partial solution of the problem of the social conscience that it gains so many adherents among the best of our young intellectuals. Into the reasons why I think it is an undesirable solution I need not go, but if man's inventive capacity had stopped with the Gilchrist-Thomas Bessemer invention in 1850 (which is when most of our social reformers seem to think it stopped) then communism would be the only hope for the future. But this is in fact not the case. Let me put in as few words as I can the present potentialities of science. In the last 150 years science has brought about a new Renaissance. Mankind is faced with the possibilities of controlling his environment on a scale absolutely undreamed of before. Every year he could be making enormous strides, for instance, towards the problem of completely removing from every individual the fear of want and fear of many diseases: of removing the necessity for ¾ of the most unpleasant labour now necessarily performed by a large working class and so on. Some of you will say 'we know all this: the progress of science is remarkable and impressive, but it leaves the eternal values unchanged. Dr Arnold's message is still true today'. But I do not think the moral potentialities of these discoveries is realised by one in a hundred of our educated men and women. They alter completely the potential social environment of our idealism and prevent its inevitable frustration. If we can hold out the possibility of the removal of a vast degraded working class then our social endeavours do not come up against a brick wall. If by the administration of vitamin preparations to every elementary school child then the general health is improved 100% we are making our equality of opportunity a more real thing instead of the slightly hypocritical sham of which we are at present rather ashamed. If by the study of genetics we can get definite evidence about the inheritance of certain factors we can go some way to clear up the problems of the intelligence and instinctive behaviour of coloured races and not come up against the racial ignorance and prejudice that is a permanent humiliation and frustration of Christian administrators. The study of the chemistry of substitutes and the methods of intensive agriculture may provide the economic basis for decentralised small communities so dear to the heart of many a reformer. These are random examples of the general thesis that science could remove the hitherto inescapable difficulties in the way of reaching the society which Dr. Arnold's school was going to build. Do not say 'ah! but this is purely material'. It is in fact so revolutionary a prospect that it has opened in the material, that it makes possible a new attitude of hope in the moral sphere. Our failure in the moral field has not been primarily a lack of good will; it has been a failure of knowledge and intelligence. Our belief in the brotherhood of man has foundered on the fact that there must be lower classes to do the menial work. Even a great deal of the bad will itself – the greed or the class hatred of a Dr. Inge for example – arises from a fear of competition where competition need not exist.[125] The New Jerusalem requires a material fabric of plenty, of health, of light, of cleanliness, of racial knowledge for its basis. The new Renaissance puts that material fabric within our grasp. Our good will need no longer make furtive withdrawals about slaves or working classes or niggers in its demand for the new life for we are on the edge of new knowledge.

What did Dr. Arnold teach of this new knowledge? Nothing. What do we teach of it? Next to nothing. The failure of our schools to seize upon the new knowledge and become its pioneers has meant the constant violation of the first of Francis' cardinal principles – that a school must have an idealism related to its social environment. By their steady refusal to grasp the significance of the changes in a civilisation rapidly developing the techniques of science the schools have frustrated themselves and the society which looks to them for moral and intellectual leadership. This frustration has occurred in a number of ways.

First, the boys have realised that the ideals absorbed in a school have apparently no meaning on that world because they know so little about that world. They know more about the economic resources of the Roman Empire than of the technical resources of their own. It is not that the idealism they receive is bad: it is because it is designed to operate in vacuo. The technological advances going on around them create a world the roots of which they do not understand and do not wish to understand and with which they cannot deal.

The second kind of frustration is that of learning itself. Because out of touch with the new world learning has looked back wistfully not forward hopefully. The study of the classics has become a barren textual game not a revolutionary adventure. The study of philosophy (as witness the slightly bewildered writing of R.G.Collingwood) has become a sterile analysis.[126] This must inevitably be so when the clerks refuse to be aware of an intellectual movement already in being. It was not so in Greece or at the Renaissance. Then learning was an adventure in a young world. There was hope and purpose in thinking, talking, making, doing for there was a long future. Could we but realise it that position is far more the case today. That realisation would revivify the whole field of intellectual endeavour.

Thirdly the failure of education to reckon with the new knowledge has led to the frustration of science itself. The New Jerusalem is built on a very distant hill – much further off than it need be. Why? Because scientific research is directed unsocially. It is scientific but it is not humanist. The storing[127] of biological research, the freezing of socially valuable patents, the abuses of science occur because the exploitation of science is unlinked with social morality. And, (and I believe this to be a most important point), this must inevitably be so while our intellectuals and our schools ignore or minimise the extent of the scientific revolution. Dr. Arnold saw, and I think rightly saw, the foundations of morality in the schools. But we have neglected to see the moral implications of scientific advance. It is suggested that many intelligent people dread the advance of science for will it not be put to devilish ends? It is the attitude of the Bishop of Ripon who wants a suspension of scientific research for 10 years.[128] Ten! He would have been safer if he had said ten thousand if he is not prepared to work out his morality in terms of a scientific society. Of course science will be put to devilish ends as long as the very people who are supposed to be fighting the devil are ignorant of the most elementary facts of the new knowledge. Of course the new Jerusalem [is impossible] when its builders are ignorant of the existence of the tools the use of which it is for them to direct.

Thus I believe that the malady of our sick schools and our sick society is a frustration through ignorance of the social potentialities of science. What is the solution? What are the concrete proposals I want to make? This is obviously an extremely difficult question to answer, and if you find my answers particularly inadequate I do not want you to condemn my whole thesis on that account. There is no more difficult task than the proposal of definite educational reforms even of the simplest sort. To lay down educational lines that shall lead straight to the New Jerusalem is not within my powers and I would emphasise that since the realisation of the problem is so recent then these suggestions are necessarily vague. Also it must be realised that a great deal of most valuable reform has been carried out though perhaps without a very clear idea of the nature of the problem.

Firstly, then, the attitude of the teaching staff must alter. Like Francis I believe that the unconscious effect of the master's whole attitude to life and knowledge is incalculable. For that reason it is not surprising that the social results of an educational institution are unsatisfactory when an intelligent member of its staff could say 'My dear Eric, you have to realise that stinks is merely an ornament'. Don't think that I am being trivial, that it all arises from a hurt professional pride and an inferiority complex. The attitude of polite tolerance combined with placid ignorance among[129] the top thousandth of the population has got to be placed against its historical background for its full calamity to be realised. That our whole scale of educational values is awry can be realised by a tiny experiment. If in a gathering of my colleagues I said that all I remembered of Greek was that Euripiedes [sic] had written the Odyssey an awkward hush would probably greet my self revelation as an ignorant fool. If I said that all I remembered of science was that water was a mixture of oxygen and hydrogen, or was it nitrogen? – it might pass for an amusing confession. Both sets of facts are meaningless . An ignorance of either the composition of water or the art of Euripedes shows a wider ignorance of subjects each of which may well be indispensable for the development of a proper view of society. But what can we do? You say 'Do you expect us all to start reading Hogben?' And I might well answer you – for I am encouraged and rightly encouraged to read Zimmern, or Tawney, or Gore, were it not that what I really want is that more nebulous and more difficult thing, a new attitude.[130] It is surely a small thing to ask that men engaged in teaching boys in preparation for the world shall set themselves to know something of the forces that are changing that world at every moment.

Arising from this is, of course, for more popular science – not of the sensational press kind but of the solid instructive sort.[131] No single daily paper has regular scientific articles – there is no demand. The Times tells us of progress in literature or art or squash rackets or nickel but not of plastics or alloys that might change the face of Britain. Until we have this kind of general popularisation as distinct from sensationalism of the Blue eyed 25 old Cantab smashes atom type, no proper social awareness of scientific problems is possible.

This will be led up to by the introduction of my next requirement – the obvious one that more science should be taught in schools. I do not necessarily mean more hours on physics and chemistry for everyone, though I think that will come and we shall be able to teach more slowly and with better results. I certainly visualise a spread of science to much lower age groups in the form of observational work on natural history or astronomy or mechanics. But more than actual time on science is a different technique of science teaching. Blame here certainly rests on science teachers and in extenuation I would only plead that science teaching is of very recent growth, and that the atmosphere of public schools has scarcely been favourable to it. But the fact remains we are not teaching in the best way from the point of view of scientific humanism and great changes have got to come about of too technical a character to consider here. In general I would say that the emphasis has got to be laid whenever possible on [and] as heavily as possible on the social significance of scientific facts. Both the kind of social background that gives more use to a certain kind of scientific discovery and the potentialities of those discoveries for mankind must be stressed. This is a very difficult task. It means the scientist becoming partly historian and the historian partly scientist, a hard but immensely profitable interfusion. A question that certainly will be asked is 'Why is it necessary for all people to learn science?' Admittedly the direction that society is taking is determined by scientific forces but what is the relation of this to teaching all boys that acids turn blue litmus red?

The immediate answer to the last question is 'very little'. It is extremely difficult to a see a direct social relationship in the elementary facts of say chemistry, just as it is very difficult to see the Roman contribution to civilisation implicit in the principle parts of arms. These facts are accepted as the necessary steps to be passed. And I would defend the teaching of science to all boys simply because only through knowledge can come realisation of power. Quite apart from other educational values which science teaching may have, it is surely more important in a scientific world that every boy should know some science than he should know some Latin. Even if he never goes very far as many boys never will, he will have a map of the country through which research is taking us. He will not feel himself in the grip of forces quite beyond his control from which he shelters in amused tolerance or pure obscurantism. If it is true that some scientific knowledge is desirable for a just appreciation of the possibilities of social advance then at least every person with any likelihood of bearing considerable social responsibility should have that knowledge.

As to the effects of the scientific renaissance on other subjects in the curriculum I am not competent to speak. My tendency would be to encourage a subject like Greek, the cultural relations of which are with a humanist and renaissance spirit rather than one like Latin where apparently they are not. The most profound effect on other subjects will be in teaching techniques where changes already coming about are signs of an increasing awareness of what our education needs. I refer of course to changes which substitute research methods for purely factual teaching and in general a free questioning adventurous spirit for one which too readily accepts authority. Further if we are get the maximum social effect from our teaching I think our general educational policy may have to be modified in two important directions that I can only mention now. We have to be more prepared to say what use a subject is in the world, use being defined as calculated to make men better. That a perfectly useless subject may be a proper study is a modern heresy and may lead to the extreme attitude of saying, 'No use at all, thank God'. Secondly we will I think have to take up an attitude of greater openness about the social applications of our teaching. We have become too afraid of being 'doctrinaire or tendencious' that our teaching suffers from a cold paralysis induced by sitting for too long on too many fences. It is pathetic [to] hear a preacher speaking on some social evil to stop shuddering on the brink of committing himself to the advocacy of sweeping constructive action for fear of being political. A good deal of teaching is of that kind. When a subject has a direct bearing on our own problems we hesitate to analyse its relevance in terms of action. It is an attitude of timidity and unwillingness to act on thought that communicates itself to boys all too infectiously. I mention it here because this kind of indecisiveness will rob the teaching of scientific humanism in particular of a great deal of its relevance and force, and I think that it can be safely replaced by more honest statement of opinion provided always that a wide tolerance is preserved.

Do I really expect these apparently minor changes in education to have a great effect on society? I am afraid that I am optimist enough to believe that they will. Let our governing class (for to be honest that is what they are) go out from the public schools, some with real scientific knowledge, all with a vision of what science could do if it was given firm direction, and let them become business men and judges and civil servants, (though it must be observed in passing that is almost impossible for a trained scientist to pass into the first grade of the civil service). Let this happen and very great changes will occur. I need not say that in my view those changes must be towards a socialist economy as being the only one that ultimately can fully exploit the resources of science. But that is a personal judgement. One thing is certain: that given the demand for a full application of the potentialities of science, and the shape of society will have to fit that demand.

But the final question remains. This is material. The moral will have to be there; and how can science escape that fact? I have already said something of this. But I would urge again that neither the development of science or of society can be healthy when science and social morality are divorced by ignorance at school level. And I would argue with all my heart that of course the moral will must be there. It is often there but directionless. An ideal of scientific humanism – the knowledge that it is at any rate partly in our own power to put the world right – will give the will, this lacking direction, will imbue it with a new idealism, will reinforce it with the knowledge that we are not in an old and decaying culture but a young one. It will send our young men out strong in the confidence that the world is not simply going to do things to them but that they are going to remodel it: that they will wring from it for the first time the material pre-requisites of the good life. If my Platonic assumption seems too naif that man will choose the good if he knows it, we can at any rate be sure that a man who does not know it has not even the chance of choosing it.

Appendix 2: Eric James and a belief in the afterlife

Letter from Eric James to Nonie Wintour 22 July 1951[132]

My dear Nonie,

When you ask in your letter, "What do you think has happened to Gerald?" you set us the most difficult of all questions. I would give a great deal to dodge it, and leave it unanswered – but I don't think that would be very honest, because I think that you do expect some kind of answer, and I suppose there is always the chance that some sentence by someone may make life a little more tolerable for you.

I ought to say two hard things at the start. The first is that I don't know the answer to your question; the second that I don't believe in personal immortality as that phrase is humanly understood.

But both of these answers need qualification.

The first very obvious qualification is that every personality has immortality, in the sense that all other personalities are different through its existence. Put in its crudest form, you are a different person through having had Gerald, and that difference, transmitted through you and other people, is undying. You are also a different person through having lost him; I even think there's something in those consolations that sound so smug, and that some people (though by no means all) are better people, more tolerant, sympathetic and loving through having had some apparently overwhelming and pointless pain like yours. At any rate the world is quite irrevocably changed by the fact of every human existence, and because Gerald was an interesting, happy and delightful person, it is changed for the better. There is one quite definite immortality – and I think if you read the first section of Day-Lewis' poem A Time to Dance, you would find this put in a way that might help you.

But perhaps it won't help you much for you quite reasonably want a more substantial hope for some future. Here I don't think that we can avoid talking in very vague terms about the nature of the universe. I do think that the very difficulty of philosophy is a help here. It is just as naïve an over-simplification to say "X is non-existent because of what has happened to him" as it is to believe in a hereafter peopled by our friends exactly as they were when we knew them. In fact, the relations between the material world and the thinking minds that know not only it, but so much else now appears to us so complex that it is possible to believe in the possibility of some sort of continuity of mind or personality just as we are beginning to believe once more in the material universe as an external object. It would be a bold person who could now say that they were certain that a whole personality was inextricably associated with a particular body. It is simply a problem that man must batter away at.

In the Phaedo (which I believe it would help you to re-read soon) Socrates, faced with this question, tackles it first from one side, then from another, and retires defeated – in the sense that he had no certainty, but confident and content because of the supreme value of that act of attacking it with courage.

You may well say "my poor good man, you simply do not know what it is like; you are treating the loss of part of myself as an intellectual exercise." And it's true that it was probably easier for Socrates to be courageous about his own death than if he had lost one of his children. But nevertheless I can only for me say that we know so little about words like eternity, or matter or existence that even if we are not Christians, it is altogether wrong to accept too easily the view that death is complete finality.

There are no words or ideas or kinds of knowledge that can repair your loss; but I do think that you can believe this – that when you say "I have a memory of him" or "I can think of him and know that he had many qualities that were not just physical ones" [-] when you say things like that, your words may have a meaning that is far greater than we can realise; I think such phrases may imply possibilities that must always be hidden in mystery, but may all the same have some comfort in them.

Well, that is the way my own ideas go when faced with your question. I wish with all my heart that I felt some confidence that they would be of the slightest help to you.

With all my very best love,
Eric

Appendix 3: Speech by Eric James to Northern Heads Conference in the presence of Hugh Gaitskell and the Opposition Education Team, October 1954

The Grammar Schools and the Labour Party

I want to begin with one or two words of explanation – and the first is in the nature of an apology in advance. It is no good bringing our distinguished visitors into the wilds of Westmorland and then not being frank with them. The value that a meeting like this may have will only be fully realised if we all speak our minds in our own way. The topic on which I am speaking is obviously one on which I feel very strongly indeed and the combination of deep conviction and the necessity to be both brief and honest may easily lead me to appear dogmatic if not offensive, and I hope that our visitors will forgive me in advance and realise that if I am sometimes vehement it doesn't mean that I am any the less aware of the welcome that is due to our guests or of the gratitude that we all feel for their presence. There is one other preliminary point that I should make. I am speaking tonight as someone whose politics are, shall I say, to the Left of centre. I think it is important to say that because what I shall aim to do in a necessarily superficial way is to show that there is nothing incompatible between the ideals which our visitors hold and the vision which many of us in the grammar schools try to keep bright.

Let us then look at the grammar schools today in the light of the Labour Party's policy. It is perhaps important to realise that they are many of them fairly recent in origin. Most of the schools represented in this room are creations of the 1902 Act. Not a few are products of the inter-war years. All of the schools represented have had their scope and purposes modified profoundly as a result of the social changes of the last 50 years of which they themselves are to some extent the architects. It is certain to say that most of the creators of the 1902 Act scarcely realised what a profound era of convulsion in our National life it heralded. Perhaps only Morant himself and the Webbs realised the full implications of the measure that was both a cause and a symptom of social change. From the developments of the last 50 years the grammar schools have emerged with three clear objectives before them.

The first is the most fundamental. In so far as we can ever dissociate educational and social function, it is the one that we can most properly describe as purely educational. It is the inculcation of right standards of judgment; the introduction of our pupils to the best ideas that men have had; to hold a mirror, however distorting, to truth; to be the agents, in short, of sweetness and light. About that function I will say nothing. To many of us, and to none more than to you, Mr. Chairman, it is in this side of their work that the ultimate justification of the grammar schools lies, and it is because many grammar schools have been not altogether unsuccessful in these tremendous tasks that you may regard them as worthy of defence. But although to those of us who believe in it, the dissemination of culture in Arnold's sense is the most compelling task of all, it is not one that secures universal approval, and still less universal comprehension. It is too nebulous, and requires too much interpretation to be the subject of party programmes. Mr. Deakin would be, I suspect, as suspicious of these of our aims as he would be disapproving of the amount of unpaid overtime worked by our staffs who carry them out.[133] I will, therefore, move on to the discussion of two other functions of the grammar school capable of more precise assessment and involving fewer judgments of value.

The first of these concerns the supply of expert manpower. When Morant was devising the Act of 1902 he realised that one of the main functions of the new grammar schools would be to attempt to meet the needs of a new society for teachers, for administrators, and for highly trained workers generally. He could not envisage, for no one could, how overwhelming those needs would become. For not only was society changing; science was opening new horizons of terrifying immensity. The developments of technology in the past twenty or thirty years, developments proceeding at an ever-increasing rate, have produced a totally new man-power situation. The two seminal fields of development in our life-time – I refer, of course, to nuclear studies and electronics – open the prospect of an industrial and social revolution potentially far more remarkable than that of the 13th century. You may hate the prospect of the brave new world. I think I do myself. But we are committed to its exploration. And that commitment demands a proper emphasis on the higher education of those with good brains in the interests of national survival. It may well be that the limiting factor in what we call progress may not be in physical resources, but simply in the number of people capable of being educated to the level required for the kind of tasks our kind of society increasingly demands. Nor is it only the technological revolution that thrusts this problem of expert manpower upon us. It is the social revolution that the Labour Party approves and of which it is in great part the inspiration. Sir Waldron Smithers can view with equanimity a semi-feudal, agricultural community with a low standard of life.[134] A socialist cannot. The urban industrialised Welfare State demands an increasing number of skilled administrators, of professional men, of welfare workers, and so on. It demands above all high productivity. We can see the impact of this man-power crisis in, for example, the Barlow Committee of 1945. It called, you remember, for a doubling of our university science faculties and an increase in arts faculties. Since that time the universities, by heroic efforts and a considerable expenditure of public money have almost doubled in size. But where have the undergraduates come from? From the sixth forms of grammar schools – their only possible source, and there the efforts have been no less heroic if not so heavily subsidised. Have the grammar schools responded to this social and economic challenge?

The answer is plain. In 1910 the grammar school of which I am headmaster had 55 boys in the sixth form, of whom 12 were scientists or mathematicians. In 1953-4 it had 433 in the sixth form of which 248 were scientists or mathematicians. Something similar has happened in other schools. What do those figures mean? They mean that if ever institutions had tried to adapt themselves to social needs, then the grammar schools have done so. We have not failed; yet we are condemned. But they mean something further: that if we abolish those schools, some of them but recently getting into their stride, the only schools that understand at all the needs and responsibilities of sixth form work, we run the risk of impoverishing at its source this supply of trained ability on which all else depends. Even now we realise its significance all too little.

You may say but why are grammar schools necessary to produce these highly expert pupils? Surely America has shown itself able to make great technological strides without grammar schools? The answers to that are complex and too long for me to set out in detail. I would remind you that considering its size and its wealth the American contribution has been rather at the technical than the fundamental level. But I would point out that because of its riches America is able, perhaps, to prolong the period of adolescence to a degree that we could never afford. Our economic position is such that we must not only educate our best brains well; we must educate them fast. But above all, I would remind you of the alarm with which Americans are contemplating the deficiencies of their educational system. I would ask you to read the important survey of the American Manpower Council, and still more would I remind you of the wistfulness with which prominent American educators regard the English grammar school. And hence we are led to the crux of this stage of my argument. They are going educational concerns; they have shown themselves capable of meeting with astonishing success a series of totally new demands for highly educated man-power. Can we consider it expedient to do anything but encourage them in their efforts? Can we, having regard for the economic interests of the country, regard it as a justifiable risk to destroy them and replace them by types of school that many of those most qualified to judge regard as incapable of fostering ability to the same degree? There is my first question.

Such a step would only be anything but irresponsible if there were some over-riding social necessity to justify it. And here I am led to the third function of the grammar schools, the promotion of social mobility. It is, of course, something that not everyone would regard as a proper function. But it is none the less an inescapable result of the grammar school system, particularly when it is combined with other educational measures such as the provision of university grants, and with general measures of social betterment. Dispassionately considered the changes in the provision of opportunity for talent in the last 50 years or even much less are truly astonishing. At the beginning of the century for a boy from a really poor home to get to a university was the result of a rare conjunction of quite outstanding ability and very good luck. Now it is a commonplace. We cannot too often remind ourselves of exactly what is meant by the fact that 3/4 of the students in our greatly expanded universities are in receipt of help from public funds. From my own school something like 140 boys have gone this year to various universities, about 50 of them I think to Oxford or Cambridge. They range in social background from the son of a strip metal worker to that of a company director. They are alike in one thing; they were chosen by merit. Every man in this room can tell a similar story. We have moved into a new world. The intellectual potential of the working classes that the left-wing public school man used to demonstrate by glowing stories about the glories of his W.E.A. class is now shown much more prosaically by the fact that his son may be kept out of Balliol by the product of Mugthorpe grammar school. And, of course, some of that stream of grammar school boys now going on to the university are becoming civil servants and scientists and business executives and technologists. We are seeing a diffusion of power that can only spring from the provision of educational opportunity to the whole community. That pregnant moment in English history when the civil service was thrown open to competition could only acquire its real significance with the development of the free grammar school. But the opportunity we provide will only be a reality if it is a genuine opportunity. It must not be an emasculated substitute for the real thing. It is unrealistic to talk of equality of opportunity. The opportunity provided by Mugthorpe will never be the same as that given by Winchester; certainly not in our time. But do not let us wilfully magnify the inevitable differences by making Mugthorpe not even a grammar school at all. The scales are weighted enough as they are. The fact is this; we who work in the grammar schools know that we have created instruments which are not altogether powerless to remedy the inequalities that environment provides. We know the problems of some home backgrounds, the drabness, the narrowness, the lack of culture. And even that we can do something to mitigate by our societies and journeys and scouts and games. But with all the difficulties, we see in our schools the greatest hope of enabling the possession of power to be associated with the qualities that alone can make that possession morally justifiable.

If what I have been trying to say so far has any truth in it one would expect the grammar schools to be the pride and hope of the socialist party. These, they might well say, are the means by which the expert manpower is being produced that alone can make the socialist welfare state a possibility; these are the nurseries of the scientific ingenuity which alone can put the material background of the good life within the reach of all; these in their accessibility are the solvents of class division and class privilege, the means by which the levers of political and economic power are placed for the first time within the reach of those best fitted to wield them, irrespective of their origins. One might, in any case, expect that education in general would be the subject of the most careful and expert study and appear as one of the strongest and most considered points in the Labour party's programme. That, I think, is what one would expect. What do we find? We find, and here I must speak frankly, enmity, ignorance, and frivolity. Those are hard words, but I believe that they are true. The enmity to the grammar schools is shown by the constant affirmations that the comprehensive school is the only acceptable form of secondary education, by the policy of the L.C.C. [London County Council] and other Labour-controlled L.E.As [Local Education Authorities], by articles such as those in The New Statesman that affirm that the grammar school cap is a greater danger than the old school tie, and in many other ways. The ignorance is shown, for example, by remarks such as those in the House that Eton & Harrow (and even Manchester Grammar School) are comprehensive schools. The frivolity is demonstrated by the educational sections of Challenge to Britain. For is it anything less than frivolous to put forward as a serious programme realisable in 10 years something that is administratively unworkable and which combines in an admittedly ingenious way the disadvantages of every other system of secondary education; a plan that is light heartedly discarded in the face of a breath of criticism; a plan that could be explicable as the result of a paper-games session at a Fabian summer school, but as a policy for education, the service that lies at the heart of a socialist society, is unthinkable.

It is very important that we should attempt to see the reasons for this state of affairs. If the grammar school is to survive we must ask ourselves why it is unpopular with the Labour party. I can only tonight discuss some of the possible reasons. First, there is on the trade union side the fear that the child from the working-class home becomes declassed by a grammar school education. This is a genuine and to some extent comprehensible fear, and it rests upon an unconscious belief in a rigid class structure in which the working-class child of ability must remain in that state to fight its battles. It is essentially a conservative doctrine. The provision of that educational ladder of which the grammar school is the most striking embodiment, does produce some great problems in, for example, the field of trade union leadership. But one has only to put this doctrine in its naked and logical form of 'we do not want working-class children to move into the professions' for it to be rejected by any socialist who is amenable to reason at all, though some such view is quite properly tenable by a writer like Mr. T. S. Eliot who fears a too fluid society. The very fact that the argument is used at all is a tribute to the success of the grammar schools in promoting social mobility.

A much more weighty argument against the views which I am putting forward is that the grammar school produces a new class structure based on ability, and that the grammar schools must be destroyed in their present form because they are the enemies of a classless society. This is a very powerful argument indeed. Are we not producing a managerial class, separated by income, habits, tastes from the herd they lead, because they are segregated from them at the age of 11+. How can the civil servant, packing his Proust on the way to week-end at his cottage, possibly legislate for the clerk or the docker reading his Reveille in the housing estate? Without going too far into very interesting sociological speculation some rejoinder must be made. In the first place what do we mean by a classless society? If we mean a society in which there is some kind of economic equality between occupational groups then that is not an educational problem and we are in any case moving towards it in the sense that a face worker earns more than nearly any of our staffs and a bus conductor as much as an assistant lecturer. If you mean a society in which no occupational or social group is given more prestige than another I doubt whether you ever will attain it, as witness the examples of two cultures at the opposite extremes, Russia and America, both of which aim at classlessness. It is probable that the way to eliminate such class-consciousness as exists in this country is to bring together individuals of different classes but similar interests.

But actually the creation of a genuinely classless society is outside the scope of the schools; it goes much too deep for that. The reason why there are 79 old Etonian M.P's[sic], 78 of them Conservative, and only 3 from Manchester G.S., all Labour, has very little to do with the schools they come from. It has a great deal to do with the homes and the social background. The idea that the schools can produce by themselves a certain social structure rests to a great extent on an overestimate of the power of the school. What education can do is to promote social mobility, particularly of the most able, and it can do something to promote tolerance between different groups. To both of these objects I would submit that the grammar schools make a great contribution. The fact that we must not over-emphasise the part played by the schools in producing social attitudes is shown by the Labour Party itself. Stafford Cripps, Attlee, Crossman, Pritt, Mr. Gaitskell himself were all educated in schools that were not only intellectually but socially highly segregated communities. Yet that has not prevented any of them from showing in their different ways a sense of solidarity with the less fortunate of their fellows.

The third reason for the dislike of grammar schools by the Labour Party is the distrust of the whole idea of selection. To some extent this is a capitalisation of the middle-class resentment at not being able to buy their way into a grammar school as they were able to do until quite recently. To some extent it rests on a laudable, if often sentimental and misguided regard for the primary school child faced with the first of life's hurdles. There is a good deal of demagogy in this and some truth. But we must try to be honest; there must inevitably be some kind of selection in the education of children, for schools can never be equal in merit. Whenever more children want to go to a school than that school has room for, we must select. Let us consider the remark of that able socialist writer on education, Miss Peggy Jay: 'our boy is going to his father's old school, Winchester, but Kidbrooke sounds an ideal place for the girls.' For the boy to go to Winchester his father must have an income of, say, £2000 a year. Even given this somewhat drastic selection he still [has]only a 1 in 8 chance of admission, and the further selection process will depend partly on his intellectual ability, partly on his father being an Old Wykehamist, and partly, say, on the fact that his prep. school regarded him as being a promising leg-break bowler. If she seriously considered sending the girls to Kidbrooke the selection procedure would be simpler: the Jays would have to go to live in a particular fairly small area of south-east London. In place of these procedures the grammar school says: 'From the children over a pretty wide area everything is irrelevant for admission to this school except the intelligence of the child.' We replace selection by the purse or by nepotism by the ability to profit from the education given in a particular school. I can sympathise with the resentment of parents who would afford to pay, but, as I say, where you have a school, whether it be Winchester or Kidbrooke or Mudford grammar school to which more people want to send their children than there are places for, then we must select on some principle. And for a socialist to object because selection is for the first time carried out in terms of ability alone seems to me almost the most extraordinary feature of the baffling educational situation in which we live.

A fourth argument against the grammar schools is that, though they promote social mobility, they do not produce it fast enough. Reports like that of PEP [Political and Economic Planning] on the class-structure of university population, and to some extent the recent work of Glass [Richard Victor Glass] on social mobility seem to show that the working-classes are statistically insufficiently represented in places of higher education.[135] Are the grammar schools still too much middle-class or at any rate lower-middle-class schools? To some extent this is possibly true. But free grammar school education is a plant of recent growth. It cannot accomplish a complete social reorientation in a generation in the face of heredity which is always with us, and environment which only a long process of social reform can modify. All it can do is to offer an equal opportunity to all in so far as any purely educational device can do so. It can seek ways to alleviate the lot of the child from the poor, the narrow, the uncultured home and all these things the grammar school tries increasingly and not unsuccessfully to do.

The final ground for the Labour Party's rejection of the grammar school rests on a rejection of the validity of selection techniques. This is largely a matter of machinery and I shall not dwell upon it. The nature of the selection examination and its fallibility have been much misrepresented often for dubious purposes. The myth of a child's whole future depending on one panic-filled day, the absurdities of some intelligence tests, all these have been magnified. Of course selection procedures are not perfect. We must mitigate their imperfections by research, by an increasing reliance on head-teachers' reports, by the facilitating of late transfers, by a blurring of the divisions between kinds of secondary school, by all the means familiar to us all. But the fact remains that in a good authority a group of head teachers of all kinds of school will tell you that they are reasonably satisfied with the results of the selection techniques, even as at present practised.

Let us turn from these negative aspects of the Labour party's policy, its rejection of the grammar school, to its more positive contribution. Its official policy is to establish in place of grammar schools comprehensive high schools throughout the country. Let me be perfectly clear at this point. In some rural areas, where educational opportunity is in any case limited, there is a case for comprehensive schools. In urban areas, or anywhere where a grammar school exists and has shown itself to be viable, I believe that case to be fallacious. The purely educational objections to the comprehensive school have been reiterated so often that I will not attempt to repeat them. They obviously make no impression whatever. And it is significant that the propaganda for Kidbrooke has been concerned more with its furniture than with what will go on there. The parties of M.P's[sic]. have been taken round an empty if striking school and shown the wonders of the internal telephone system, for as an L.C.C. pamphlet explained 'the central problem of comprehensive education is the rapid diffusion of information.' It is significant too that the team of speakers who have devoted themselves to the public justification of the comprehensive idea has not been one of teachers; it has been one of administrators. As an administrative and architectural unit Kidbrooke is probably a triumph. So, if Dante is to be believed, is Hell. Whatever justifications Kidbrooke may have they are obviously not purely educational ones. It is not, therefore, on educational grounds that I wish to examine the comprehensive schools, but on social ones. Is it more or less likely that a grammar school can contribute to the social ends which the Labour party and most of us hold in common? It is claimed that by avoiding separation into different schools at eleven it will help to create a classless society. This seems to me most improbable. Is it seriously contended that if children from widely different homes, in which after all they spend nearly 4/5 of their lives, after having been educated during the impressionable years of 5 to 11 in common primary schools, and being faced with the prospect of 2 years of common national service, are educated between the ages of 11 and 15 in a single building, though in quite different streams, the social gulfs that still persist will be bridged? Even if they are educated in the shadow of the largest Venetian blinds in Europe that seems a somewhat naif assumption. It may, indeed, be reasonably contended that such an organisation of secondary education will accentuate rather than diminish social segregation. Large as they are, such schools must be drawn in urban districts from fairly small geographical areas. Lady Simon, one of their ablest defenders, actually says that they are likely to be most successful in homogeneous social groups such as are found on new housing estates. If Manchester Grammar School went comprehensive tomorrow its class mixture would be far less complete than it is now, for it would draw on a housing estate on one side and a fairly good residential neighbourhood on the other. Gone would be the son of the miner and the weaver, the boy from a back street in Oldham who now works with the son of the company director from Altrincham. The focus of this localisation upon social prestige in American high schools is well described in, I think, Barzun's book, 'Who shall be educated?' And in America where the comprehensive high school is supreme, could anything be more naked that the plutocracy that exists? And if you say 'Ah, but things would be different here,' all we are really saying is that social tradition and the whole spirit of a society has far more influence than the schools upon the class structure. If, indeed, the comprehensive school could produce a classless society, whatever that is, it might conceivably be worth the frustrations and inefficiencies it will bring. But a classless society is something that will not be won as easily as that. The devils of division are the sort that are only exorcised only by prayer and fasting.

The second argument I will bring today against the comprehensive school may seem technical and trivial. It is really fundamental and as far as I know has never been properly discussed. It concerns the supply of teachers, and is most clearly shown as regards science teachers. As we know there is a shortage of science teachers; some of us have been mentioning it since 1945 and it has now reached the stage of a Ministry pamphlet and an F.B.I [Federation of British Industry] committee.[136] It is actually so important a problem that I am not exaggerating when I say that the future prosperity of this country is bound up with its solution. What has this got to do with comprehensive schools? Let me explain in the simplest possible terms. I have a very good physics master. He spends his time teaching my very good sixth form physicists who are going to give this country a lead in nuclear physics, or jet aircraft, or computing machines. Because mine is a selective school, they form a large group and take nearly all his time. If the Labour party secures power and turns Manchester Grammar School into a comprehensive school a great part of his time will be spent in teaching very elementary general science to average or below average children. 'But how good for him!' it is said. 'How good for them! How it will extend his sympathies! How it will broaden their horizons!' That might well be true if there were many such men. But there are not: there are very few. We cannot, we dare not, diffuse their energies on those who cannot derive full benefit from their rare abilities or pay the maximum dividend afterwards. The number of academically gifted teachers is so small, particularly in science, and always will be, that we must concentrate as far as we can the children that they alone can teach. Yet the whole philosophy of the comprehensive school explicitly states that all teachers shall teach all streams. Even if it did not, the concentration of talent must be so small that these teachers must be wastefully employed. If I were convinced by every other argument for the comprehensive school, this alone would be decisive. I should realise reluctantly that the needs of our national economy that alone can make socialism possible must lead to the rejection of the comprehensive principle. One comprehensive school can succeed; two may succeed. But as a universal principle they are doomed to failure. They will be wrecked on one particularly dangerous rock of that whole reef that threatens our kind of society - the shortage of skilled manpower. Only by careful concentration of talent can we hope to survive the shortage of academically first-rate teachers. If we reject the comprehensive principle what then is a rational educational policy for Labour? This is not really for me to say, but I would emphasise that it will probably be an unspectacular one. The necessary improvements in primary and secondary modern schools cannot be dramatic. Even if Labour is prepared to put at the service of education more money than a Conservative government, ultimately progress must rest very largely on the quality of the teachers. It may well be that the Labour party should be devoting more time and thought to an examination of the relationships between central and local government and the individual school, so that the sense of liberty and responsibility of the individual teacher may be increased. It might well be contended that much more should be done to subsidise sixth-form work so that the gap between the £70 a year that the State spends on a boy in June and the £700 a year that it is prepared to spend when he goes to a university in October is to some extent bridged. But whatever else it does I am urging tonight that the grammar schools desperately need and richly deserve the confidence

of the Labour party, and far more than any legislative change we desperately
need a public expression of that confidence for the encouragement it would
bring. The recruitment of their teachers, the way in which they face their
problems, which God knows are difficult enough, the idealism and vision that
they bring to their work, all these are menaced by the knowledge that they
are in jeopardy from the very party that should most applaud their efforts.
That is the case which I hope will emerge from this week-end's discussions.
Let me sum up: there are three points that I want to leave in your minds.
The first is that the grammar school is a reasonably flourishing educational
institution. It includes many schools that are good schools, however that
word is interpreted. Are good schools of any kind so easy to create that we
can afford to destroy them by absorbing them in institutions whose major task
seems to be the overcoming of the gratuitous difficulties that they themselves
create? Secondly, the grammar schools present the only answer that we know
by experience to the problem of training the expert manpower that our age
and our society increasingly demand. Their record shows that they have
been astonishingly successful in meeting an unprecedented challenge. With
encouragement and support they would be still more so. Alternatives to them
are in the opinion of those teachers most likely to know less likely to be
capable of supplying an adequate education for the abler children. Dare we
then, at this most critical time in our economic history, at this particular phase
of scientific development, embark on an experiment at best dubious, at worst
well-nigh fatal.

Lastly, and perhaps most important, we would maintain that the grammar
schools are justified on social grounds. I spent last night at Eton. I reflected
then with envy, as I always do, on much that I know that great school gives
to its pupils. But one thing I do not envy. I can come back to my own school
and know that its doors are open to any child who has the intelligence to
pass them. No wealth, no position, no family association can secure a boy a
place. A selection there must be, and of a rigorous kind. We are saying that
since more boys want to go to a grammar school than the grammar schools
can or should accept we will select them on grounds of intellectual ability.
The Labour party is saying that since these are schools to which not everyone
can or should go, then no one shall go and they must be wiped away. The
very instruments we have created to give the boy from the working-class or
lower-middle-class home the chance to acquire by his own merits some of
the powers, to see some of the visions, to sieze some of the opportunities that
Eton offers so richly, these are what have been called schools of privilege,

these are what the Labour party has voted year after year to destroy.

Let me be frank. There are in this room 40 or 50 men who care about education and who have some experience of it. It is not a gathering of Conservative teachers or a political assembly at all. There are those here whose lives are devoted to the State system of education because they believe in that system; because, with all its imperfections, they believe that only through the intervention of the State can the liberty that rests on opportunity be realised. Yet it is a lamentable fact that to those very men, whatever way they may vote, the prospect of the Labour party in power, with its present educational policy, offers not the hope that it should, but rather the menace of ill-considered policies, of the denial of opportunities, the lowering of standards, and the frustration of legitimate hopes. For those of us whose sympathies have always been on the left it is a humiliating and bitter thought that the advent to power of that party whose lifeblood should be educational advance is something that is feared by the most highly educated section of the teaching profession. There is the fact; I have stated it baldly; I have given some of the reasons that lead us to it. There is nothing that I for one would welcome more than to be made to see that all our fears are groundless.

Appendix 4: Hugh Gaitskell's diary entry of his visit to the Northern Heads Conference and his response to Eric James' speech in Appendix 3[137]

I spent the weekend in the Lake District, in a hotel with the grammar school headmasters of Lancashire and Cheshire. The purpose of this was principally to discuss the Labour Party's proposals for education, and in particular the comprehensive school. The person who I think suggested that I should be asked, and indeed, probably started the whole idea of the Conference, was Eric James, the Headmaster of Manchester Grammar School.[138]

I had not met him before, but he has made a great name for himself in education. He was a don at Winchester before going to Manchester, and is nevertheless still, I think, only about 45. Alice Bacon and Michael Stewart came with me, and we had a weekend's pretty solid discussion.

The headmasters began in somewhat truculent mood, and I was rather astonished to hear them say, one after another, that the Labour Party was against the grammar schools, that it had attacked them, that it was trying to destroy them, etc. James himself, in what was obviously a deliberately provocative speech, said our policy was based on 'ignorance, frivolity and enmity'. He made, however, some telling points, the most important of which, I thought (and it came up several times during the weekend), was the fact that in some areas to start a comprehensive school, instead of the present division between secondary modern and grammar schools, would in fact lead to more not less class division. You would get a residential area on the one side, where there was a comprehensive school and all the people there would be drawn from the middle or lower middle classes. On the other hand, you would have a working class area, and equally there all the children would come from working class parents. This would be in contrast with the present situation, whereby in the grammar school itself, owing to the fact that the places were free and that entry was on merit, there was now a complete mixing up.

The other argument was, of course, the fear that in comprehensive schools the bright, clever children would be at a disadvantage. They would not get the same specialist teaching, and the stream of boys and girls to do the professional jobs requiring more brains would suffer in quality.

We put up between us quite a good case, I think, for the comprehensive school, and criticised the grammar school on the grounds (a) that half the boys and girls in fact left at about 15 or 16, so that the argument that they were being trained for something higher simply did not apply, (b) that the proportion going to grammar school differed from 50% in one area to 10% in another, so that the character of the grammar school varied enormously, and they could not be defended on the same arguments. We argued also that provided we were prepared for fairly large schools there was no reason why bright children should suffer, and that there was really no case against fairly large schools, e.g. Manchester Grammar School and Eton. We pointed out that in the main segregation at 11 did lead to a class structure, whereas what we wanted was more social cohesion.

I think that by the end of the weekend we had begun to understand each other's point of view better. My own feeling was that we should not be too precipitate in this matter because of the many local problems that would arise (we had some good contributions on this from Directors of Education), and that only if our programme had been phased in a little more wisely, we should not have had nearly so much hostility from grammar schools and other people in the teaching profession, as well as some of our own Labour Education Committees.

Appendix 5: 'Eric James: From The Corridor' by Alan Garner[139]

"It's yer school, and yer responsibility." The eminently imitable exhortation with which Eric James would so frequently berate Morning Prayers was the affectionate hallmark that boys used to define his High Mastership.

Now Eric James is dead. The obituarists have had their say, and judgments will be formed. What I should like to attempt here is to show how his life and philosophy influenced that of others at the level of the school corridor. It will be subjective, personal. It is not hagiography. Yet such was one man's influence on so many boys, each of whom could tell their own different story, that I suspect that the overall tenor would be the same, whoever were to write this piece.

The early accounts must be anecdotal. It is the fate of an outstanding teacher to be promoted away from the art of teaching, and, at M.G.S., the result is that the Lower School boy and the High Master, unless there should be trouble, are unlikely to become intimates.

My first view of Eric James was that of all: the slight figure who greeted us (if "greeting" can ever be the word applied to the emotions of that moment) in the lecture theatre on our first day. I was struck immediately by the quality of his eyes, which remained for me the most subtle and devastating item in his armoury. With them (I was to learn) he could inflict a delicate nuance and also quell a mob. They were eyes that could face fourteen hundred boys and make each boy feel that they were only looking on him.

At the end of the week the Chief took an English lesson unannounced. He asked us to write our impressions of the school. I devoted my time to an excoriation of the desks, and asked how, since they were already too small for me, I could hope to endure the effect of them on my physical growth during the next seven years. After half an hour, Eric stopped his pacing, swept up my essay at random and leant against the window. He read the lesson in silence, and then looked at me; and he launched into a detailed analysis of the Receiver's problems during the Second World War (it was then 1946) and an explanation of how, although my plaint had been long recognised, there were priorities, and I could well end up, as I did, having to accommodate my frame to the torture of wood and iron for the rest of my days as a pupil……..But the important impression left with me was that the Chief had taken me seriously and had addressed himself sympathetically to a First Former as to an equal. It was a hint of the man…..

In my second year, I was standing one day with my arms open, at the top of the steps leading down to a forbidden basement outside the Paton Library. A cold voice said, "What are you doing?" It was a most sceptical Chief. "Thinking, Sir". He changed instantly. "Good" he said, "Forgive the intrusion."……

Such glimpses built up over time, meant that by the Sixth Form…..I had a picture of a man of total intellectual honesty, a relentlessness of brain and will, which were the product of continuous reassessment of belief and thought, who held that the highest, and for him, only, pursuit was the development of individual potential to its fullest, in the cause of excellence and the service of humanity. …..

Eric James would stop at no lengths for "his" boys, but, in return, with a kind of innocence, he expected adherence to his precepts. A boy was automatically assumed to be self-motivated, ambitious in the best sense, and, by the Sixth Form, to have shaped some direction to that purpose.

Not every boy responded, or had developed so far at that age, and Eric James was not unequivocally popular with all. Later, men have told me they found him cold and remote. Some have said they had no sense of being in control of their destinies….My own memory is that his clear goal, the result of complete integrity, could make him appear inflexible, when confronted with ideas he did not respect, or that were incompetently presented. His pursuit of academic achievement (never an end in itself, despite his critics' claims) made him, in my opinion, neglect artistic achievement in the School. But money and the timetable would go only so far, and he would always listen to advocates of change, even though his reply would be, say, to the suggestion of the introduction of glass-blowing. "Yes, but in place of what?"

I feel that this seeming high-handedness was, in origin, sometimes disappointment at human frailty, and sometimes exasperation that a clever boy had not used the School to its fullest and thought his way forward. Far from being a rigid autocrat, my experience of Eric James (and I have many times witnessed this) is that one of his greatest pleasures was to be forced, by intellectual ingenuity and persistence to change his mind. If an argument was inelegant, he would say, in order to be clear, not discourteous, "You're wrong," and leave it at that. But if a boy did not leave it at that, his patience was infinite, until a smile would come over his face, and he would concede with a characteristic chuckle of delight. He was a wholly generous man, full of humour (at the parties he and Cordelia gave for prefects, we were expected to mime "Antidisestablishmentarianism" or "Einstein's mass energy equation"), with a proper arrogance born of true humility. He often said that the supreme reward of teaching was to realise that he was teaching a boy more intelligent than himself.

And the supreme reward of being taught at M.G.S. was to be taught by Eric James. His time was restricted, but this Fabian agnostic took upon himself the Religious Instruction of the Sixth Form. What we got was an awesome trip through the history of Western Thought, after a thoroughgoing grounding in Platonism. The Chief bemoaning the while his ignorance of Classical Greek. The method, inevitably, was by Socratic dialogue, conducted at a lope, his gown swirled to make every point, every trap set by a twinkling of the eye and a trailing off of the voice into a dangerous, "You see?..."

His concern for religion did not stop there. About the least sought duty of a prefect was to read the Lesson each morning for a week. The choice of text was a matter for the individual, but, on the Friday before our practice in public speaking, we each had to justify our selection before the Chief.

When my turn came, I was more than at a loss. For me, then, knowledge of The Bible was restricted to the reading of Mark in Greek; and my first brush with God had ended at the age of four, when I had broken away from the tocsin of the Sunday school bell and run home, yelling, "I am fed up with that Jesus Christ!" So in desperation I solicited a member of one of the more evangelical groups at school.....who happily supplied me with five extracts from the Book of Revelation, and presented myself at the High Master's study.

The Chief heard me out. Then he said, "Do you belong to a sect?" "No, Sir" "I suggest you spend the weekend in some other areas of the Bible," he said, "and let me have the list on Monday morning before nine." As I closed the door, thoroughly rumbled, he said, "Try 1 Corinthians 13, for a start, and see what you think." And it was that text that prepared my mind for the possibility of becoming a writer.

When that writing did happen, years later, after National Service and Oxford, I met Eric James by coincidence as we occupied stalls in the urinal of Kendal Milne. "What are you doing, besides the obvious?" he asked. Now it is possible to say, "I have written", but it is not possible to say, "I am going to write". The pretentious words can't be spoken. Yet those eyes were on me, and they were very blue in a way that I recognised, "I am going to write." I said. "All right, then, write," he said. "I always hoped I'd get one."[140]

Eric James is dead. I do not miss him. It is just that, with his going, everything has become more important. He formed me. Without his example,

I should have had no model on which to build a positive and uncompromising life. And what he did for me, he will have done for generations of boys. We are all in his debt. His work has reached into every field of human concern, through his clarity of thought and his ability to imbue that of others. It is an act of highest creativity. I do not miss him. What he was, in the effect he had on boys of his High Mastership, and what they have passed on to the world, he still is and will be. He gave us ourselves. It is our school. It is our responsibility.

Appendix 6: University of York Promotion Committee

MEMORANDUM TO THE UNIVERSITY GRANTS COMMITTEE

Contents   Page

December 1959

1 INTRODUCTION

This memorandum is presented to the University Grants Committee by the York University Promotion Committee, which is a representative body appointed solely for the purpose of preparing and presenting the case for a University of York. The Committee represents the City of York, the three County Authorities of Yorkshire, York Academic Trust, the C. and J. B. Morrell Trust, the Joseph Rowntree Memorial Trust and the Joseph Rowntree Social Service Trust.

The idea of a University of York is not new -- there were petitions to James I in 1617 and to Parliament in 1652, and in 1947 a deputation from the City of York was received by the University Grants Committee. There has probably never been more enthusiasm and more support than there is at the present time.

2 UNIVERSITY EXPANSION

The Report of the UGC on University Development 1952-1957 estimates an increase in the number of full-time students at university institutions in Britain from 94,600 in 1957 to 124,000 by 1965, with the possibility of a further permanent increase of 10% by 1970.

We understand that in order to meet this demand the UGC is now examining the possibility of recommending the establishment of new university institutions. In the sections which follow we give the reasons on which our claims to a university are based.

3 WHY YORK SHOULD HAVE A UNIVERSITY

York's claims to a university rest on its unparalleled historical continuity, its physical and cultural amenities, the availability of a site and accommodation, the advanced educational institutions already established there, and local support, particularly the financial support already promised by local trusts.

(a) Physical Amenities

It is the best centre of communications in the country, and is readily accessible from all the principal cities - for example, London, Bristol, Liverpool, Glasgow, Edinburgh. The land immediately surrounding the city is flat, and would be suitable for the future development of air transport.

It is a historic county borough, and the population of the city and its immediate district is about 125,000. It is surrounded by an agricultural belt and yet is within easy distance of the coast, and of the large industrial areas of the West Riding, the Tees and the Humber. Its situation makes it, along with its own varied industries (chocolate, railways, scientific instruments, building, glass and printing) and extensive medical services, an admirable centre for sociological and some scientific research.

York is one of the most beautiful towns in the country, and possesses much of the ethos of Oxford and Cambridge. It has fine buildings, a good river and rich unspoilt countryside close at hand. It still provides the necessary peace for scholarly study but is at the same time a community fully representative of mid-20th century life.

(b) *Cultural Amenities*

From the time of the Romans until the present day -- with particular high lights in the time of Alcuin, during the middle ages and in the 18th century -- York has been a cultural centre, as well as the northern seat of civil, religious and military government.

It maintains this cultural tradition today. There is the Minster, with its religious and musical life, and its library; a civic theatre; musical and other societies; a thriving art gallery; the collections of the Yorkshire Museum, with its gardens and library, and of the Castle Museum; a number of important independent schools and a variety of flourishing secondary schools with substantial sixth forms; a technical college of 4,500 students, now being provided with new buildings; and a substantial amount of extra-mural activity by the Universities of Leeds and Hull. There is also an important triennial festival of the arts.

York's heritage from the past attracts thousands of tourists each year. The less superficial and more intangible aspects of that past would draw students on a large scale (as has already happened on a small scale) from all parts of the English-speaking world.

The archaeological, historical and architectural survivals from the past make it an admirable centre for research in, and teaching of, the traditional humanities. But possessing all the administrative machinery and both public and voluntary services of a great city on a scale small enough to be readily comprehensible, it can also make a valuable contribution to the study of subjects like government, both national and local, and sociology -- what may, in fact, be called the humanities of the 20th century.

York could attract a cosmopolitan range of students and provide them, not only with the basic material for teaching and research in many branches of learning, but also with the aesthetic and intellectual inspiration for higher education in its widest sense.

(c) *Site*

There is a magnificent main site available at Heslington (see maps on p. 11), forming a wedge coming right into the city and presenting a wonderful opportunity for the architect and landscaper. Seventeen acres, including Heslington Hall, are already owned by the Joseph Rowntree Social Service Trust, and negotiations are in progress for the purchase of a further 137 acres adjacent to the Hall and extending inwards towards York as far as the limits of the site. Immediately to the west of the site there is common land (Walmgate Stray) owned by York Corporation and used as playing fields. Heslington is exactly two miles from the city centre or the railway station. No other city has a virgin site so near to its centre, where there would be no undesirable segregation of university from civic life. For state and ceremonial occasions, there are notable buildings within the city walls: in particular, the medieval Merchant Adventurers' Hall and the 18th century Assembly Rooms of Lord Burlington yield in distinction to no secular buildings in the land.

Apart from such residential accommodation for students as might be built on the main site, it would be possible to convert for initial temporary use part of the army barracks at Fulford, just across Walmgate Stray, if they become redundant within the next few years. We are confident that accommodation for students in private houses in York could be provided.

(d) Financial Resources

It appears that the two most recent university institutions are so far being financed almost entirely from public funds. Any institution set up in York would also rely heavily on public funds, but York is well placed to attract funds from other sources, thereby relieving pressure on the public purse and strengthening the independence so vital to an academic institution. Its reputation, as Oxford and Cambridge have found to their great benefit, would attract funds from overseas, and it is most fortunate in possessing important charitable trusts with considerable financial resources and sympathetic to educational projects. Furthermore, there is already in existence an independent body, established for this very purpose, with funds of its own.

(e) Steps already taken towards a University

The deputation from York which met the UGC in 1947 took, as a result of the advice then given them, the first steps towards their objective. From that time until the present, the effort to create academic institutions of the highest quality has been continuous. We believe that no other city has done such a thing. The independent body which carried out this work was at first an academic development committee of York Civic Trust, but in 1956 became an independent and legally established charitable institution under the name of York Academic Trust. Its achievements are summarised in the following section.

4 YORK ACADEMIC TRUST

Up to 1958 the Trust has raised on capital account £60,000. When a life annuity on a major endowment falls in, the capital sum will become £90,000. Some £31,000 has been expended on the conversion and equipment of two buildings, and the remainder is in income-producing investments.

Between 1950 and 1958 the Trust has had an aggregate income on revenue account of £65,000, consisting of grants (mainly from the Joseph Rowntree Social Service Trust), income from investments and students' fees. This has been spent on the administrative expenses of the Trust, the establishment costs of the Institutes, and on courses.

The growth of the Trust's activities can be judged by the increase in its annual expenditure from under £2,000 in 1950 to nearly £13,000 in 1959.

Before reviewing its work in more detail, it is noteworthy to record tangible recognition from one of the older universities in the form of a capital gift of £1,000 from King's College, Cambridge.

(a) Borthwick Institute of Historical Research

The Institute originated from summer schools in 1949, and became established as an Institute in 1953. It is housed in the medieval St Anthony's Hall, which is owned by the York Corporation, who spent £5,000 on restoring its fabric and then granted the Trust a long lease at a peppercorn rent. The Pilgrim Trust gave a grant of £12,000 for its equipment, and further grants in 1958 and 1959. Its main endowment, which will eventually amount to £60,000, was given by the trustees of William Borthwick.

The Institute contains the archives of the archdiocese of York, Church Commissioners' records and other documents: in all, more than a million documents. There are facilities for research (with or without supervision) and a library. Short courses are held. Scholars from all parts of the country work there, with others from abroad (chiefly the USA).

The Institute was awarded grants of £4,500 by the Leverhulme Trust in 1954 for research on the ecclesiastical courts of York and of £1,600 by the Carnegie United Kingdom Trust in 1957 to catalogue its archives. Its Director, Canon J. S. Purvis, DD, was awarded the OBE in the 1958 honours' list.

(b) The Institute of Advanced Architectural Studies

This also originated from summer schools in 1949, and became established as an Institute in 1953. Since 1956 it has been housed in the former medieval church of St John, Ousebridge. It was converted and equipped for £17,000, most of which was raised locally by public appeal, but included £1,000 from the Pilgrim Trust and £1,000 from the Historic Buildings Council. An endowment appeal is now in progress.

The Institute's chief work is the provision of courses at post-graduate level for members of the architectural and allied professions. It is a pioneer and unique venture, which has attracted the support of all the national societies and official bodies concerned. Courses for students and laymen are also held. There is a valuable and rapidly expanding library of books, photographs and slides, and also research facilities. Students come from all parts of Britain and overseas, from Poland to Australia and the USA.

The Institute was awarded a grant of £2,800 by the Carnegie United Kingdom Trust in 1957 to establish a national reference centre for protection and repair of historic buildings. In 1958 it received a donation of £500 from the Cassell Educational Trust. Its Director, Dr W. A. Singleton, has been appointed Hoffman Wood Professor of Architecture at Leeds University for 1959-1960.

(c) Other Activities

Annual courses for overseas students on the British way of life have been held, in association with the British Council, since 1953 and attended by students of university level from many parts of the world, such as Japan, Ghana, Austria and Malaya.

St Anthony's Press, which issues the publications of the Institutes, was established in 1952. It has so far produced five books, seventeen booklets, nine bulletins, and the Trust's annual reports.

At present the Trust is investigating, jointly with York Corporation, the possibility of establishing in the King's Manor a college for senior officers in local government, with research and teaching at a high level, and provision for comparative study of problems on an international plane. An informal approach has been made to the Association of Municipal Corporations, the Ministry of Housing and Local Government, and the County Councils' Association.

5 IDEAS FOR A UNIVERSITY OF YORK

In general, we visualise a university providing teaching and research facilities in both arts and science; governed by a Court, Council and Senate; and granting its own degrees from the start.

We should like York ultimately to have a collegiate university. The universities founded since the mid-19th century appear now to be destined to expand to a size which, had it been foreseen at their beginnings, might well have led to the adoption of the collegiate system. It is accepted that where large numbers are concerned, the collegiate system provides a greater opportunity for each student to express and develop his personality. And there is a widely held opinion (difficult to substantiate by quotation, as it rarely figures in speeches and similar pronouncements)* that Oxford and Cambridge owe much of their pre-eminence to this system, and that any new universities, were it financially possible, ought to adopt it. Since our university would be founded in a city whose environment for this purpose we believe to be second only to Oxford and Cambridge -- and since it is by no means improbable that its establishment on collegiate lines might attract far greater endowments than would otherwise be the case -- we ask that this possibility be examined.

The factors governing our choice of subjects for study have been the desirability of ensuring fruitful interaction between the arts and the sciences, and the substantial contribution we believe York could make in the field of social sciences. Basic subjects to be covered might be:

ENGLISH LANGUAGE AND LITERATURE, HISTORY,
MODERN LANGUAGES, PHILOSOPHY, MATHEMATICS, PHYSICS,
CHEMISTRY, BIOLOGY, ECONOMICS, SOCIAL SCIENCE

An Institute of Education, including some of the training colleges in the region, would be desirable at an appropriate stage in the University's development.

We believe that a University of York could have a special opportunity of fulfilling a particular role and fusing something of the spirit of older education into the study of the modern community and its needs. We are giving much thought to the forms which this might take, but meanwhile we mention certain fields of study where immediately the possibility would seem to be considerable.

(a) **Administration** in all its forms. The increasing complexity and spread of bureaucracy in modern life calls for constant research and enquiry into administration and theory of government. Local government, industrial and social welfare (particularly in view of the pioneer work carried out here by Seebohm Rowntree), business administration, transport, and communications touch us all in our daily lives and should be made the subjects of special study.

(b) **Architecture** The development of the pioneer work at post-graduate level of the Institute of Advanced Architectural Studies, also bearing in mind the suitability of an accompanying undergraduate school of architecture.**

*but cf. letter to The Times (7 October 1959)

'...Why then are no new collegiate universities founded? Surely the way to save Oxford and Cambridge from being swamped is to make other universities as much like them as possible. Will Brighton, York, and Norwich, for instance, have the collegiate system? If not, why not?'

** There are, in all, too many schools of architecture at present, but it can be argued that there are not enough at university level. Cf. RIBA Journal, November 1959, pp.4-13, Report of the Committee on the Oxford Architectural Education Conference.

(c) **Landscape Architecture** The only full-time undergraduate course in the country (that at Reading University) is to be discontinued in 1962. There is clearly a need for more full-time university courses, and York would be particularly suitable because of the wealth and variety of landscape and geological conditions surrounding it, and the tradition of instruction in this subject already built up by the Institute of Advanced Architectural Studies.

(d) **History** The development of the work of the Borthwick Institute of Historical Research, and its unique collections of archives.

(e) **Archaeology and Music** These two subjects are marginal to present national requirements but are particularly apposite for York. Both York and the surrounding area are rich in archaeological material, and the Yorkshire Museum contains important exhibits and a good library. There is a strong musical tradition in York, based on the Minster and the various musical societies.

(f) **Overseas Students** The number of overseas students continues to increase (11% of the total in 1957). York is a microcosm of the British way of life and, as existing courses have shown, has much to offer them; and particularly to students from the Commonwealth who will later become leaders of their countries when they attain self-government, and replace more primitive ways of life by new systems modelled on Western democracy and technology.

We conclude this section by giving our reasons for the omission of certain subjects. The applied sciences and technology would involve a major development at great cost, and are better studied in industrial areas.

Medicine is omitted because there is at present no national need for more schools in this subject.

6 CATCHMENT AREA

The development of modern transport and of a fairly uniform system of university awards throughout the country have progressively ensured that most universities now draw their students from a very wide area of the country and can no longer be called local universities. In this connection the remarks made by Dr R. P. Linstead at the Home Universities Conference in December 1958 are pertinent:

'It is sometimes said that universities should be set at appropriate distances apart and should correspond to definite spheres of influence and in regions which are historical and cultural entities. This argument has a good historical basis, but it derives from the days of bad communications and has rather a stagecoach flavour. It is, of course, true that when a community of about the right size is largely isolated, even under modern conditions, as for example in Northern Ireland, there is an obvious need for a university which has, in fact, a very real and important regional significance. But under present conditions in the United Kingdom, the importance of this factor is diminishing. I believe that the movement of students is to be encouraged; and is in itself a great educational force. In its extreme form we have the admission of overseas students, a very desirable thing. The trend of statistics shows that a regional attitude is on the wane among students.'

By virtue of York's unique attractions and facilities, which are widely known, the University would draw students from all parts of the United Kingdom and the English-speaking world.

7 COSTS

At this stage only an approximate idea of the costs of a university in York can be given.

As regards maintenance, the annual cost might be £800,000* with 2000 students. In the initial stages (when the cost per student place would be relatively high) the annual cost might be £80,000 with 150 students.

Capital costs of building are even harder to estimate, since they are so dependent on the range of subjects studied and the proportion of residential accommodation provided, but the total for York would obviously be very substantial.

It is confidently expected that the capital costs of the site will be met from local resources.

*This has been calculated by calculating the average expenditure per student place at some of the newer universities (expenditure at London, Oxford and Cambridge is not comparable) as given in the UGC Returns from Universities and University Colleges 1957-58, published in September 1959.

	Total number of students	Expenditure	Expenditure per student place
Exeter	1,189	£384,989	£324
Hull	1,303	£433,899	£333
Leicester	923	£352,976	£382
North Staffs	644	£303,773	£472
Nottingham	2,337	£1,038,758	£444
Southampton	1,407	£510,858	£363
Average			£386

2000 students @386 = £772,000 add for rising costs £28,000 = £800,000

8. LOCAL SUPPORT

If local contributions towards the annual maintenance costs of the university are expected to be on a scale similar to that at the newer universities, then these contributions will represent about 10% of the total. (The percentage for the years 1957-58 was 11.4.) **

** UGC Returns...

Percentage of total fee income from parliamentary grants, student fees and government departments for research.

Exeter	88.8
Hull	89.4
Leicester	92.1
North Staffs	84.5

Nottingham   85.0
Southampton   91.8
Average percentage 88.6
Income from endowments, donations, grants from local authorities, and for
research from bodies other than government departs.
Average percentage 11.4
Total 100.0

It is not possible to produce similar percentage figures for local contributions
towards capital expenditure, but it would appear that during recent years
capital costs (except for residential accommodation) have been paid by the
government.

At the present time the list of local contributions is incomplete. It is not
possible to estimate what the total value of these contributions, either in the
form of capital donations or recurrent grants, will be.

York Corporation has declared its intention to support the project. Until
the outcome of negotiations for the site is known, the Corporation will not be
in a position to state the extent of its financial contribution.

There has not yet been time for the three County authorities to consider
to what extent they will be able to give financial support, but they have
expressed their interest and goodwill and have arranged to be represented on
the Promotion Committee.

Such contributions as can be listed, however, are given below:

(a) from York Academic Trust
The entire assets of the consisting of:
  (i) The Borthwick Institution of Historical Research (£7,200 spent on
       restoration and £5,000 on furnishings) with its library and staff.
  (ii) The Institute of Advanced Architectural Studies (14,500 spent on
       restoration and £3000 on furnishings) with its library and staff.
  (iii) Property and investments of some £36,000 producing
       approximately £2,500 pa. A further £30,000 will added to the
       endowment on the death of a life annuitant at present aged 71. The
       Trust also hopes to augment its financial contribution as result of
       an endowment appeal for the Institute of AdvancedArchitectural
       Studies now in progress.

(b) from the C. and J.B. Morrell Trust
The trustees have decided they would like to make available to the York

University when established the sum of £100,000, to be contributed at the rate of £10,000 a year for ten years. They would also like to discuss and agree in due course with the University authorities the nature of the work and the purpose that this should endow.

(c) from the Joseph Rowntree Memorial Trust
The trustees are prepared to contemplate a contribution of £100,000 at the rate of £10,000 a year for ten years to assist in a general way in the establishment of a University. Furthermore, in the light of the developing situation, they would, on agreed conditions, be prepared to contemplate ways and means of providing substantial additional support, in the right way and from time to time, in the specific field of social sciences along the lines of the Trust's powers and interests.

(d) from the Joseph Rowntree Social Services Trust
The trustees undertake to transfer to the new University, when established, Heslington Hall and grounds and to make a contribution of £150,000 spread over the first ten years, divided as to about one third for the general work of the University and the maintenance of existing institutes within the University, and about two thirds for the development of specialist and advanced studies. The exact form and proportions of the contributions will be subject to agreement in consultation with the University authorities when established in due course.
In addition, we confidently expect considerable financial support from local industry.
At an appropriate stage we envisage a public appeal on a national and international basis, and we are confident that this will be successful.

The extent to which existing and future offers can be used most fruitfully towards capital projects or, alternatively, for endowment cannot be ascertained at this stage. It is for this reason that no sub-division of present contributions into capital and revenue (although some may be restricted one way or another) has been made, but in principle we should prefer that, in so far it is possible, contributions from private or independent sources be accumulated as part of the University's general endowment fund, or the endowment funds of specific faculties or departments. In this way we should from the start we should possess a degree of financial, and hence academic, independence proportionate to that enjoyed at present only, we believe, by Oxford and Cambridge.

9 CONCLUSION

This application has the united and wholehearted support not only of those representatives who submit this document, but also of other societies, trade organisations, private individuals and the like, too numerous for individual mention.

We believe there now exists an opportunity to create in York a university institution of distinctive character and of high cultural significance whose contribution to and reputation in the national, and we hope international, field of higher learning will be as much by virtue of its quality as by its quantity.

Appendix 7: The Appointment of Lord James as Founding Vice-Chancellor

Once the UGC had decided to found two new universities at Norwich and York, their first move had to be the setting up of Academic Planning Boards to oversee the process of establishing the new institutions. The model adopted was that previously used successfully in the case of Sussex and which Sir James Duff (Vice Chancellor of Durham) had chaired.

In the case of York it seems as if the UGC and Sir Keith Murray were keen on the appointment of Lord Robbins as the Chairman of the York Academic Planning Board from the outset. The University of York Promotion Committee was similarly supportive, and William Wallace particularly so in his role as member of the Promotion Committee and as Chairman of the Joseph Rowntree Memorial Trust, a position he had held since 1951. Wallace had joined the York Academic Trust in late 1956 as he was about to stand down as Chairman of the Rowntree Company. He quickly became active in the discussions about how the campaign for a university in York might be furthered and what role the Rowntree Trusts might play in securing a university. In particular, he was keen to encourage the development of the social sciences in York, building on the traditions of the Rowntree family and the later Trusts. It is not clear if Wallace already knew Robbins personally, but he would certainly have known of his academic reputation from his own interests in the role of the state in relation to business. A year before in March 1959 Robbins had submitted a draft report to the JRSST on 'York University and Advanced Institute in relation to existing institutions and new development', just at the time that the YAT was preparing for its informal meeting with Murray at Bishopthorpe in June.[141] By the following year, with the UGC's decision to go ahead, Robbins had joined the JRSST himself under the chairmanship of J.B. Morrell. On this basis Wallace pressed for Robbins appointment as Chairman of the Academic Planning Board. Given the significance of the Rowntree Trusts in securing the successful outcome of York's bid, Murray did not put any objections in the way, even though convention suggested that an existing Vice-Chancellor should take on that role. The result was that Murray had the potentially delicate task of securing Sir William Mansfield Cooper's (Vice-Chancellor of Manchester University) agreement to serve as Deputy Chairman, something Mansfield Cooper willingly accepted, later explicitly praising Robbins to Murray for the care and energy he devoted to the role.[142]

With Robbins as potential Chairman, the UGC had to consider who would join him on the Board and a speculative list was discussed twice at the UGC's monthly meetings early in 1960. Among names suggested were Mansfield Cooper and Lady Ogilvie (Principal of St Anne's College, Oxford) to reflect a commitment to undergraduate teaching and to represent the interests of women students, but the name of Lord James of Rusholme was also included, James having left the UGC himself after ten years membership at the end of 1958. However by the time of its meeting in April 1960, Lord James' name no longer appears.[143]

After a certain amount of negotiation the membership of the Board was finally agreed as it was about to hold its first meeting on 6 October 1960, with its immediate task to start the process of drafting a Charter and Statutes to submit ultimately to the Privy Council and to appoint a Vice-Chancellor. Among names considered earlier in the summer was that of Roger Wilson, strongly supported by William Wallace. Wilson, Professor of Education at the University of Bristol, a member of a number of Quaker Trusts, was unavailable.[144]

The members were: Lord Robbins (Chairman), Sir William Mansfield Cooper (Vice-Chancellor of Manchester University), Lady Ogilvie (Principal of St Anne's College, Oxford), Sir William Hodge (Master of Pembroke College, Cambridge), Sir Francis Hill (Chancellor of Nottingham University) and Professor J.H.Wilson (University of Leeds), Secretary: John West-Taylor (University of York Promotion Committee)

During September as the Academic Planning Board was preparing for its first meeting in October, Mansfield Cooper was in correspondence with Sir James Duff and John Fulton on governance issues as experienced at Sussex, and whether Durham was a suitable collegiate model for York to consider.[145] Duff thought Durham was not a relevant model. He also began preparing a document for the Board suggesting how the governing structure at York might enable non-professorial staff to engage in the broad development of university policy, a scheme that reflected what was subsequently approved by the Board a year later as the university's Professorial and General Academic Boards.

At its first meeting on 6 October, the Board agreed to submit suggestions to Murray as to a potential vice-chancellor and also to invite nominations from the Vice-Chancellors of Oxford, Cambridge and London, the Cabinet Secretary, the Head of the Civil Service and the Permanent Secretary at the Treasury.

By 3 November a list of 35 names and curriculum vitae had been collected for its meeting in York two days later. They included that of Lord James. In the surviving type-written copy of that list among the Mansfield Cooper papers are annotations added by Mansfield Cooper in a few cases. Against the name of James is that of Wallace. At this and the subsequent meeting of the Board on 24 November a non-minuted discussion took place on the progress made in selecting a vice-chancellor.[146]

At this point the written and oral record runs out until 3 December when Mansfield Cooper writes to Robbins to tell him that he has seen James and that he, James, would be prepared to meet the Committee. Two days later, James came to York to meet John West-Taylor and visit the Heslington site, which he later described in rather lugubrious terms. As far as is known no other person on the list visited York. Certainly John West-Taylor in his own accounts never mentioned any individuals, other than James viewing the site.[147]

On 6 December Robbins wrote to James to invite him to 'friendly discussions' with the Committee in London. Robbins added that they were, not surprisingly, considering a number of other suggested names. At that meeting James was almost certainly asked if he would consider an invitation to become the first vice-chancellor.[148] While it was no doubt the case that the Board had a short list of possibly acceptable other candidates, there is no surviving evidence, as far as the author knows, that anyone else was approached, visited York or was invited to 'friendly discussions in London. About to go on a speaking tour in Nigeria James asked for time to consider and to give a reply in the New Year. By his own account, James returned from Africa still very uncertain as to his decision. Cordelia commented that he had already been at Manchester for fifteen years, that he was getting stale and was still only 51. He decided to accept.[149]

At its meeting on 19 January 1961 Robbins reported to the Board that he had written to Archbishop Ramsey to inform him that the Board was recommending to the University of York Promotion Committee that it should invite Lord James of Rusholme to become the first vice-chancellor of the University of York.

At the meeting of the University of York Promotion Committee on 23 January, Archbishop Ramsey reported on his meeting with Lord Robbins and that he had been 'immensely impressed' by the thoroughness of the Board in considering the 35 candidates suggested and that it was unanimous in its recommendation of Lord James.

In his verbatim notes of the discussion on 23 January, John West-Taylor records that William Wallace immediately reminded Ramsey that he had suggested James, when the Committee had met the UGC in December 1959. Alderman Butterfield reminded the Committee that he had mentioned Lord James when the Board came to York, while Sir John Dunnington-Jefferson described James as one of the most distinguished men in education today and his only surprise was that he had accepted. In conclusion the University Promotion Committee agreed unanimously and 'with enthusiasm' to endorse the recommendation.[150]

APPENDIX 8: List of those suggested for consideration as a possible Vice-Chancellor of the University of York [151]

Dr. Walter Adams (1906-1975)
Principal of the University College of Rhodesia and Nyasaland since 1955.

Dr. Thomas Alty (1899-1992)
Principal of Rhodes University since 1951.

Robert Birley (1903-1982)
Headmaster of Eton since 1949.

John (Jack) Butterworth (1918-2003)
Fellow of New College, Oxford since 1945.

Professor Arthur Clapham (1904-1990)
Professor of Botany, University of Sheffield since 1944 and Pro Vice-Chancellor 1954-8.

Sir Andrew Cohen (1909-1968)
Governor and Commander in Chief, Uganda, 1952-7, Permanent British Representative on the Trustee Council, United Nations since 1957.

(J) Patrick Corbett [1916-1999]
Fellow of Balliol College, Oxford since 1945.

Professor Stanley Dennison (1912-1992)
Professor of Economics, Queen's University, Belfast since 1958.

Professor Kingsley Dunham (1910-2001)
Professor of Geology, University of Durham since 1950.

Professor Lionel Elvin (1905-2005)
Director of the Institute of Education, University of London since 1958.

Norman Fisher (1910-1972)
Director of the Staff College of the Coal Board since 1955.

(F.) Harry Hinsley (1918-1998)
Fellow of St John's College, Cambridge since 1944.

Professor Daniel Jack (1901-1984) *David Dale Professor of Economics, University of Durham since 1935.*

Lord James of Rusholme (1909-1992) *High Master of Manchester Grammar School since 1945.*

Professor Alexander Jeffares (1920-2005) *Professor of English Literature, University of Leeds since 1957.*

Professor Robert Jennings (1913-2004) *Whewell Professor of International Law University of Cambridge since 1955.*

Dr. John Lockwood (1903-1965) *Master of Birkbeck College, University of London since 1951.*

Sir Douglas MacDougall (1912-2004) *Fellow of Nuffield College, Oxford since 1952.*

Professor William Mackenzie (1909-1996) *Professor of Government, Victoria University of Manchester since 1949.*

Michael McCrum (1924-2004) *Fellow of Corpus Christi College, Cambridge since 1950.*

Dr. John Morris (1910-1984) *Fellow in Law, Magdalen College, Oxford since 1936.*

Sir Stanley Prescott (1910-1978) *Vice-Chancellor of the University of Western Australia since 1953.*

Professor Michael Roberts (1908-1996) *Professor of Modern History, Queen's University, Belfast since 1954.*

Professor (E.) Austin Robinson (1897-1993) *Professor of Economics University of Cambridge since 1950.*

Raymond Smail (1913-1986) *Fellow of Sidney Sussex College, Cambridge since 1946.[152]*

Frank Thistlethwaite (1915-2003) *Fellow of St John's College, Cambridge since 1945.*

Professor Ronald Tress (1915-1985)   *Professor of Political Economy, University of Bristol since 1951.*

Professor Claude Wardlaw (1901-1985)   *George Harrison Professor of Botany, University of Manchester since 1958.*

(Lancelot) Patrick Wilkinson (1907-1985)   *Fellow of King's College, Cambridge since 1932.*

Edgar (Bill) Williams (1912-1995)   *Fellow of Balliol College, Oxford since 1945.*

Charles Wilson (1914-1991)   *Fellow of Jesus College, Cambridge since 1938.*

Endnotes

[1]   For the background to Lord James of Rusholme's life and career (1909-
        1992), Roger Young, 'James, Eric John Francis (1909-1992)', *Oxford
        Dictionary of National Biography*, Oxford, Oxford University Press, 2004
        (http://www.oxforddnb.com/view/article/ accessed 1 February 2016). *The
        Times, 19 May 1992, Daily Telegraph 18 May 1992, The Guardian 19 May
        1992* (Anne Corbett with additional note by Sir Andrew Derbyshire, 23
        May 1992), *The Independent* (Gerald Aylmer, 21 May 1992 with comments
        by others, 23 May 1992). See also text of addresses given at the memorial
        celebration for Lord James' life at the University of York 5 October 1992,
        including Gerald Aylmer, Anne Riddell, Lord Harewood and Sir Andrew
        Derbyshire, and memorial tributes, *Ulula* (Manchester Grammar School
        Magazine) (1992), P.Nuttgens, *York University News Sheet* (June 1992),
        courtesy of Professor Oliver James. For Cordelia, Lady James, obituary, see
        Tam Dayell, *The Independent* 22 March 2007.

        For studies of Lord James: David Smith, 'Eric James and the Utopianist
        Campus: Biography, Policy and the Building of a New University during the
        1960s' *History of Education*, 37, 23-42, 2007; Gary McCulloch, *Philosophers
        and Kings: Education for Leadership in Modern England*, (Cambridge, 1991)
        pp. 70-81.

[2]   University of York, Borthwick Institute for Archives (BIA), Sir Keith
        Murray to Archbishop Michael Ramsey, 19 April 1960, Minutes of the York
        University Promotion Committee, BIA, UOY/F/YUPC/1/1.

[3]   Michael Shattock, *Making Policy in British Higher Education, 1945-2011*,
        (Open University Press, 2012), which contains a comprehensive bibliography.
        See also, Stefan Muthesius, *The Postwar University : Utopianist Campus and
        College*, (London, 2000).
        Malcolm Tight, *The Development of Higher Education in the United
        Kingdom since 1945*, (London, 2009), Harold Perkin, *New Universities
        in the United Kingdom: Case Studies on Innovation in Higher Education*,
        (Organisation for Economic Co-operation and Development, 1969) esp.
        pp.69-70.

        For accounts of the founding of the University of York, Lord James of
        Rusholme, 'The Starting of a New University', in *Transactions of the
        Manchester Statistical Society*, (1965-6), pp.1-21; 'The University of York'
        in Murray G. Ross (ed.), *New Universities in the Modern World*, (1966),
        pp.32-52; Christopher Storm-Clark, 'Newman, Palladio and Mrs. Beeton:

The Foundation of the University of York', in Charles Feinstein, (ed), *York 1831-1981: 150 Years of Scientific Endeavour and Social Change*, (York, 1981), pp.285-310.

In addition there is an extensive oral record made at various times by the founding members of the University. On his retirement as Vice-Chancellor in September 1973, Lord James gave an extended interview with Stuart Sutcliffe: see BIA, UoY/HIS/3/1/9. Stuart Sutcliffe also interviewed Andrew Derbyshire at that time. Further oral material was gathered, some of it relating to Lord James' time, as part of the University's 50th anniversary in 2013 with interviews conducted by Gregory Neale. These can be accessed at https://dlib.york.ac.uk.

Architectural historian Andrew Saint also recorded a substantial number of interviews with architects, educationalists and administrators who had worked on post-war new public buildings. Among those interviewed about the founding of the University of York were Lord James, John West-Taylor, Professor Patrick Nuttgens, Sir Andrew Derbyshire and Professor Harry Rée. These recordings are preserved in the British Library (BL), Archive of Recorded Sound, Andrew Saint Recordings File Format C447/15/01 (Patrick Nuttgens, Lord James of Rusholme), C447/34/01 (John West-Taylor), C447/09/01 (Andrew Derbyshire), and C447/31/01 (Harry Rée). Arising from this project, Andrew Saint wrote *Towards a Social Architecture: The Role of School Building in post-war Britain* (1987), which includes a chapter on Stirrat Johnson-Marshall of the practice Robert Matthew Johnson-Marshall, the University's chosen architects, with its pioneering architectural approach to public commissions. James Walsh, Registrar of the University of Leeds, made transcripts of conversations with many of those closely involved with the politics of university education in the 1960s following the election of a Labour government in 1964. These transcripts can be found in The University of Leeds Archives, Handlist 182MS 1774/1- Papers of James Walsh. In preparing for his chapter on the founding of the University by Christopher Storm-Clark above, Storm-Clark had a long interview with the founding Registrar, John West-Taylor, the notes of which are located in BIA, UoY/His/1/2.

[4]   For the setting up of the Academic Planning Board and the more detailed description of the process of appointing James see Appendix 5, including the list of those suggested as a possible Vice-Chancellor. See The National Archives (TNA), UGC 1/8 - Committee minutes 1960; University of Manchester Archives (UoM), Mansfield Cooper Ms, VCA/7/266; BIA, UoY/F/YUPC/1/1 Minutes (4/7/60 and 20/7/60). For the University of York Promotion Committee's endorsement of the appointment 'with enthusiasm'

BIA, UoY/F/YUPC/1/4 (Verbatim Minutes - 23/1/61).

[5]   The group promoting the idea of a university at York went under a number
        of changes of title. Initially named as the University for York Committee, it
        had made the first unsuccessful bid to the UGC in March 1947. In 1949 it
        became the Academic Committee of the Civic Trust, significantly dropping
        'university' from its title. It became a separate charitable trust in November
        1955 as the York Academic Trust. As the prospects for success improved,
        it changed its title again in late 1959 to the University of York Promotion
        Committee, the title it retained until it was dissolved on the granting of the
        Charter and Statutes to the University in 1963. For documentary material
        relating to these founding committees see BIA, UoY/ F/EC –Early Campaign
        Correspondence, UoY/ YAT/CT – Civic Trust, UoY/YAT- York Academic
        Trust, UoY/F/YUPC-University of York Promotion Committee.

[6]   For accounts of the York-based campaign to secure a university, see
        Katherine A. Webb, *Oliver Sheldon and the Foundation of the University of
        York* (Borthwick Paper No.115, 2009), and *City of our Dreams: J.B. Morrell
        and the Shaping of Modern York* (Borthwick Paper, forthcoming), 'In York
        the opportunity awaits, and all history beckons', unpublished lecture. I am
        grateful to Dr. Webb for her kindly allowing me to see the copies of the
        lectures on which these papers are based and for conversations more widely
        on the origins of the University. For biographical detail on Oliver Sheldon
        and John Bowes Morrell, see Webb, *Oliver Sheldon*. For Eric Milner-White,
        Fare, P., and Harris, D., *Eric Milner-White, 1884-1963: a* memorial, (London
        1965); Wilkinson, P., *Eric Milner-White, 1884-1963*, (Cambridge, 1963);
        Holtby, R.T., 'ed', *Eric Milner-White: a memorial*, (Chichester, 1991).

[7]   Leading figures included John Bowes Morrell, Eric Milner-White, Oliver
        Sheldon, Noel Terry, Arthur Rymer, B.P. Rowntree, John Shannon and
        Donald Barron. For details see Annual Reports of the York Academic Trust,
        BIA, UoY/YAT/CT

[8]   For York's submission to the UGC in March 1947: BIA, UoY/F/EC/1/1,
        UoY/YAT/MIN/1-7, and for UGC response, TNA, UGC/1/2/1947
        (24/4/1947).

[9]   John West-Taylor (1924-1991), born of musical parents, educated St
        George's School Windsor, a chorister, then at Cranleigh School, Surrey,
        before going up to Trinity Hall, Cambridge in 1942 to read music. On being
        called up, he joined the Fleet Air Arm and trained as a fighter pilot in Canada,

before serving in Ceylon. On demobilisation he returned to Cambridge, changing to history. On graduation, he followed a year-long course in palaeography, before applying for the post of secretary to the academic committee of the York Civic Trust in 1950. The author is most grateful to Catherine West-Taylor, John West-Taylor's widow, for providing information about her husband and the founding of the University in conversations on 5/6/2014 and 1/9/2015.

[10]   For York's efforts in the 1950s, BIA, UoY/F/EC/2/2, UoY/YAT/MIN/1-7.

[11]   In a discussion about the possible new universities in 1952, the UGC noted that little was now being heard from York and Brighton, although noting that an annual meeting was still held at York: TNA, UGC/1/3/1952 (17/1/1952).

[12]   For the minutes of the UGC's discussion on university numbers from 1950-56, see TNA, UGC/1/3 and 4. The emphasis was on the need to encourage students in science and technology. For instance, Dr. Eric James (a member of the UGC since 1949), emphasised in particular the need to arrest the decline in the numbers wishing to study technology as boys usually decided upon their careers between the ages of 16 and 18: TNA, UGC/1/3/1953 (12/11/1953). The assumption remained that increased science and technology numbers could be accommodated within existing institutions and that there was no need to expand numbers in the arts. But the UGC also noted that the response from existing institutions to expand in the desired areas had been 'disappointing' in the cases of King's College, London, Bristol, Newcastle and Reading: TNA, UGC/1/4/1956 (19/4/56). From early 1956 the emphasis of the Committee's discussions changed in relation to the need to expand science numbers and it prepared a paper for consideration by the Treasury: TNA, UGC/1/4/1956 (20/12/1956). At the same time, they were considering the case submitted by the local authorities for a new university at Brighton. In reply to a question from Sir Eric James, the Chairman replied that there were no other applications pending: TNA, UGC/1/4/1956 (19/7/56). The Treasury eventually agreed to set up what became the University of Sussex in the following year. For the ongoing discussions on the founding of Sussex see TNA, UGC/1/5/1957.

[13]   TNA, UGC/1/4/1956 (29-30/11/1956)

[14]   The names of the various Joseph Rowntree trusts and their changing titles can be confusing. Essentially there have been three charitable arms:
The Joseph Rowntree Charitable Trust – A Quaker charitable trust.
The Joseph Rowntree Village Trust (1904), which became the Joseph

Rowntree Memorial Trust in 1959 and is concerned with housing, social
research and development. This became the Joseph Rowntree Foundation in
1988.
The Joseph Rowntree Social Services Trust – a non-charitable trust with
democratic rights and politics at its core. This became the Joseph Rowntree
Reform Trust in 1990.

[15]   For Milner-White's pessimistic report on the correspondence with Murray see
BIA, UOY/YAT/MIN/1-7 (7/10/1958).

[16]   By early 1958, the UGC had convinced the Treasury that provision had to
be made for an increase in student numbers in addition to the separate issue
of increasing the scope of university education in the south-east through
the founding of a university at Brighton. For the evolution of UGC and
government thinking more generally, see Harold Perkin, *New Universities*,
pp.62-75. For later reflections on the tensions between expansionists and
consolidators within the Committee of Vice-Chancellors, see transcript of
conversations between Sir William Mansfield Cooper (then retired Vice-
Chancellor of Manchester University) and Sir Charles Morris (then retired
Vice-Chancellor, University of Leeds) with James Walsh, Registrar of Leeds
University, March 1977: University of Leeds Archives, James Walsh Papers,
Handlist 182 MS1774.

[17]   Norman Fisher (1910-1972), educator, broadcaster and publisher was an
important background influence on the founding of the University of York
and its first Vice-Chancellor. Early in his career he had joined the Education
Department of Cambridgeshire County Council and was profoundly
influenced by Henry Morris (see footnote 22 below). During the Second
World War he had worked closely with Philip Morris as the director-general
of army education. By 1958 Sir Philip Morris was Vice-Chancellor of the
University of Bristol and Chairman of the Committee of Vice-Chancellors
and Principals. Following a period as deputy chief education officer for
Lancashire, Fisher was Chief Education Officer for Manchester from 1949-
55. He worked closely with Eric during his middle period as High Master
of Manchester Grammar School. Both served on the Northern Advisory
Council of the BBC, which Fisher chaired; Fisher also chaired the BBC's
General Advisory Council from 1955-62. Both men were also members of
the All Souls Group (see footnote 100 below) and appeared regularly on the
television version of the B.B.C's discussion programme, The Brains Trust, of
which Fisher was the chairman. On his death in February 1972, Eric gave the
address at Fisher's memorial service. See *The Times*, 3 February 1972 p.16,
BIA, UoY/ JAM/2/1/9

[18]   At the meeting of the YAT in February 1959, the Vice-Chairman, Arthur
        Rymer, noted the recent public campaigns for new universities, examples
        of which included Brighton, Coventry and Hereford, and in which York
        had been mentioned in both *The Times* and the *Manchester Guardian*.
        West-Taylor reported that he had written informally a few weeks before to
        Norman Fisher on whether York should make an approach and had received
        an 'encouraging reply' to the effect that circumstances had 'markedly
        altered' since Milner-White's more tentative approach the previous summer.
        See West-Taylor to Sir Herbert Read, 4 February 1959 commenting on his
        approach to Fisher: BIA, UoY/YAT/Corr/10-15. At its later meeting on 17
        April 1959 Milner-White reported again that the planning framework on
        student numbers had changed and that there would not be a better opportunity
        in the next five years to make York's case successfully. It was agreed to invite
        Murray to York in the next two months for informal discussions: BIA, UoY/
        YAT/1-7.

[19]   For instance, at a meeting between Archbishop Ramsey, John West-Taylor
        and Sir Keith Murray about possible members of the Academic Planning
        Board, Murray stressed the importance of undergraduate teaching within the
        thinking of its future membership. The invitation to Lady Ogilvie to join the
        Board as Principal of St Anne's College, Oxford may have been a part result
        of this, in addition to her role as the representative for women students, BIA,
        UoY/F/YUPC/1/1 (4/7/60). For the UGC's commitment to innovation see
        Harold Perkin, *New Universities*, p. 70.

[20]   A sign of the changed times can also be seen in the UGC setting up a
        sub-committee to consider proposals for new universities: TNA, UGC/1/7
        (12/3/1959). In May 1958 the Committee accepted Sir Colin Anderson's
        report on changing the basis of student grants: TNA, UGC/1/6 (12/6/58) and
        in July it considered the growing evidence of rising demand from qualified
        candidates for admission to degree courses: TNA, UGC/1/6 (26/11/1958). For
        the Anderson report on *Grants to Students*, see Command Paper 1051, 1959-
        60. These various discussions were brought together in three draft papers
        prepared for the main UGC committee meeting in November 1959: TNA,
        UGC/ 2/56 (19 November 1959).
        1. A draft report to the Treasury in support of planning for higher student
        numbers than anticipated in the Treasury statement of 20 February 1958,
        Hansard 5th ser., vol. 582, col. 140.
        2. Notification that the UGC was considering the possibility of additional
        new universities through its sub-committee in response to local campaigns
        for a university. Coventry, Gloucester/Cheltenham, Norwich, Thanet/Kent
        and York were specifically mentioned among a group totalling 13 in all.

3. Draft criteria for assessing these local proposals. It is quite possible that John West-Taylor may have had a hand in the formulation of these criteria as the note prepared for the UGC meeting of 7 April 1960, (still before formal confirmation from the Treasury had been received in respect of York) contains quite detailed examples from York's case as a guide for others considering making a submission.

By early 1960 the Treasury had agreed a possible further increase of between 35 and 40 thousand in student numbers by 1970, and in March 1960 Sir Keith Murray reported that officials were in discussion with 14 existing universities about further expansion, with only Durham and Newcastle feeling that they had real difficulties with such an expansion, TNA, UGC/1/8 (3/3/1960). At its meeting on 7 April 1960, the UGC circulated members with a copy of the Memorandum to the Treasury on New University Institutions, recommending the establishing of two new universities at Norwich and York adding 'in that order'. This probably reflects that there was still uncertainty at York, unlike Norwich, that a site would become available: TNA, UGC/2/60 (7/4/60)

[21]   For the meeting with Murray at Bishopthorpe, see West-Taylor's briefing notes, 24 June 1959 and other correspondence: BIA, UoY/YAT/MIN/1-7 (16/6/1959).

[22]   West-Taylor notes following Murray's visit: BIA, UoY/F/YUPC/1/3 (24/6/1959). Later in the year on 19 October 1959, West-Taylor wrote a briefing note for Milner-White on 'How a University is Founded': BIA, UoY/YAT/Corresp. 1-9.

[23]   West–Taylor briefing notes 24/6/59, above footnote 22.

[24]   See footnote 3 above.

[25]   H.Ree, *Educator Extraordinary: The Life and Achievement of Henry Morris*, (London, 1973), and for a more critical assessment, Tony Jeffs, *Henry Morris: Village Colleges, Community Education and the Ideal Order*, (Nottingham, 1998).

[26]   Catherine West Taylor conversations with the author on 5/6/14 and 1/9/15.

[27]   At its meeting on 3 March 1960, the UGC considered the possible membership of the Academic Planning Board for York – a list which included the names of both Robbins and James. Conventionally, the choice of chairman in circumstances such as these was usually a neighbouring vice-chancellor. But as these were to be national institutions from the beginning,

awarding their own degrees, this was no longer thought appropriate. As a result the name of Sir Charles Morris (Vice-Chancellor, University of Leeds) was dropped, TNA, UGC/2/59 (3 March 1960).

28 The late Sir Donald Barron in conversation with the author.

29 William Wallace (1891-1976), Chairman of the Rowntree Company (1952-1957), Chairman of JRMT (1951-1963). Wallace had joined the Rowntree Company in 1919 and had worked his way up the company. He had interests in social economics, was a member of the National Birthday Trust Fund and the Acton Fund as well as being prominent in the Federation of British Industries and a founder Member of the British Institute of Management. Writer on private enterprise and the state's relationships with industry. Many years after, he revealed that he had written Lloyd George's 1929 General Election manifesto, 'We can conquer unemployment.'

30 *Who's Who*, (London, 1961 ed.).

31 Eric was born at 58 White Street, Derby. For family background, the author is very grateful to Professor Oliver James, in conversation.

32 Eric attended Brighton Municipal Secondary School (previously known as York Place Board School) from 1919-1922. On entry his address is recorded as 11 Waterloo Street, Hove, later amended to 55 Millers Road, Brighton. Later renamed Varndean School, the school is now a local authority sixth form college. Information kindly provided by Clive Henly, President of the Old Varndeanian Association-22/7/2012. The school's records are now deposited with the East Sussex Record Office. For Eric's later visit to Varndean School in 1959 see BIA, Lord James of Rusholme Ms, JAM/1/1 Speeches and Lectures, 1940-1962.

33 For Taunton's School, now Richard Taunton Sixth Form College, see Old Tauntonian website at www.ota-southampton.org.uk/history (visited 29-04-2015).

34 Final school report – courtesy of Professor Oliver James.

35 The author is greatly indebted to Michael O'Riordain, Archivist to the Queen's College, Oxford, who gave me his unique insights about the College in the 1920s and 30s as well as guiding me through the College's archive. Meeting 12/11/12. Among the teaching fellows of the period were Eric's tutor F.D. Chattaway (chemistry), Godfrey Elton (history), Oliver Franks

(philosophy).

[36]   Personal information.

[37]   For Chattaway, see obituary notice by G.D. Parkes (Fellow in Chemistry, Keble College, Oxford), *Nature*, 153, (1944) pp.335-6.

[38]   The Queen's College archives, Oxford, *The Queen's College Record* (1930).

[39]   The Queen's College archives, Oxford, *The Queen's College Record* (1933).

[40]   The Queen's College archives, *College Record Book*. Eric's fellow Taunton Scholar to Queen's in 1927 was Harold Vincent Dacombe, whose father was a clerk in a coal office, reading modern languages, again with no sporting interests and would like to be a schoolmaster. Recorded as living in Southampton in 1950. Eric was one of three undergraduates admitted to read chemistry in 1927- James Hanson, open scholar, educated at Radley, hockey player and anticipating becoming an industrial chemist, which he became as recorded in 1950, and John Shore, Hastings and Local Authority Scholar, educated at Heath School, Halifax, also an industrial chemist in 1950. The Queen's College, Archives.

[41]   Oxford University Archives, Record cards relating to the Oxford University Appointments Board, notes by interviewer of prospective graduates. Eric John Francis James, interviewed 8/11/30.

[42]   Frederick David Chattaway and Eric John Francis James, 'The condensation of Bromal and Urea', *Proceedings of the Royal Society of London*, 137 (1932), pp.481-488.

[43]   For Eric's doctoral history, see Oxford University Archives, Report of the Faculty Board of Physical Sciences in relation to the doctoral examiners report, part quoted, Reference FA 4/15/2/3/ p.195. My grateful thanks to Simon Bailey, Keeper of the Archives, University of Oxford, for providing me with this information on 13/7/2012.

[44]   Oxford University Archives, Oxford University Appointment Board interview notes. Eric John Francis James, interviewed 27/1/33.

[45]   Chattaway 1933 among interview notes in footnote 44.

[46]   Winchester College Archives E6/1, James to Stephen Jenner 10/1/1985

in response to a query from Jenner about his retrospective feelings about Winchester in the 1930s. Eric's comments on Williams are certainly unfair about a man, who had secured a Double First at Oxford, had been elected a prize fellow of All Souls, and later became Dean of Christ Church, and Bishop of both Durham and Winchester. The author is very grateful for the help of Susan Foster, Winchester College Archivist in tracking down James' material.

47   The author is grateful to the following for their personal memories of Eric James as a Winchester don: the late Irvine Watson, Major-General Stuart Watson, Mr. A.O.J Cockshutt, the late Sir Jeremy Morse, the late Gerald Aylmer and Ursula Aylmer.

48   Winchester College Archives E6/1, James of Rusholme to Stephen Jenner.

49   Author's conversation with Professor Oliver James.

50   Eric Freeman Dyson, *The Scientist as Rebel*, (New York, 2006), pp. xiv-xv.

51   For Gerald Alymer's recollections see the obituary in *The Independent*, footnote 1 and his address at the memorial concert for Eric in the University of York, October 1992, by courtesy of Ursula Aylmer. For the tradition of the weekly essay, see P.H.Travers (Winchester 1932-7) who wrote on the Italian Abyssinian Dispute for Eric James in 1936, Winchester College Archives F20/23.

52   Winchester College Archives, *The Wykehamist*, 1933, nos. 776 and 777 for reports of the Debating Society.

53   Winchester College Archives, *The Wykehamist*, 1940, no. 871.

54   For an appreciative obituary of Cordelia, Lady James (1912-2007), see Tam Dayell, *The Independent*, 22 March 2007. In that obituary, Dayell recalls that Cordelia had secured a first class degree in Classical Greats at Lady Margaret Hall, Oxford in 1934. He also noted that the distinguished scientist Christopher Longuet-Higgins had also been a pupil of Eric's at Winchester. Longuet-Higgins had described himself as 'an insufferably precocious child' who 'always knew he was cleverer than Eric'... 'But in Cordelia James I met my match. She was not a lady to be crossed.' Freeman Dyson, similarly distinguished, described her at these camps as 'a wonderful camp mother'.

55   In conversation with the author on 3/5/2013, A.O.J. Cockshutt commented

that Eric regarded Leeson as the most able man he had ever met. Cockshutt
had been in College at Winchester during the war, although not taught by
Eric. He later became a member of the staff at M.G.S. from 1954, teaching
English, until moving to Oxford as an English don and Fellow of Hertford
College, Oxford. He saw Eric as liking Winchester for its atmosphere of
'rational enjoyment'. He also commented that while the two of them differed
almost totally in politics and religion (Cockshutt converted to Roman
Catholicism along with Michael Dummett, later Wykeham Professor of Logic
in Oxford, while at Winchester), he always learned something from Eric in
talking about any aspect of his own field of 19th century English literature.

56   For Eric's appreciation of Leeson's influence on him personally, see anon,
        Spencer Leeson: *A Memoir by some of his friends* (London, 1958), pp. 60-88.
        Although the contributors to the volume are not named, this section is clearly
        written by Eric. For Butler and the Education Act, Anthony Howard, *RAB:
        The Life of R.A. Butler* (London, 1988), p.122.

57   Cockshutt describes Eric as having a Fabian approach to political, social and
        educational matters, but that he became increasingly disillusioned with the
        direction of Labour education policy in relation to non-selective secondary
        schooling. Oliver Corbett, on the other hand, who also taught at M.G.S.,
        described James as 'Fabian in method'. Oliver James in conversation with
        the author commented that he did not believe that his father was ever a
        member of the Fabian Society, while adding that at some period of his life he
        bought two copies of the *Daily Herald* in order to support the Labour Party:
        Cockshutt interview, 3/5/2013; Oliver Corbett, 'Lord James of Rusholme and
        the School 1945-61'; J.A. Graham and B.A. Phythian, (eds.), *Manchester
        Grammar School, 1515-1965*, (Manchester,1965) p.123.

58   BIA, UoY/ JAM/1/1/2 Manchester Grammar School Speeches, Scripts and
        Lectures, 1940-1959, 'Education and Scientific Humanism' 16/3/1940, (see
        appendix 1).

59   S.R. Humby and E.J.F. James, *Science and Education,* (Cambridge, 1942).
        Earlier he had written with Frederick Walter Goddard (Head of Science at
        Winchester) a school textbook, Elements of Physical Chemistry, (London,
        1938), designed for the abler school student and first year undergraduate.
        Comment by Professor David Waddington to the author, 1 June 2013.

60   Manchester Grammar School archives (M.G.S. archives), Minutes of the
        Board of Governors (26/4/1945). The five short-listed were A.W.Barton
        (HM of King Edward VII School, Sheffield), H.M.Grummet (HM of Royal

Academical Institution, Belfast), K.B.Webb (HM of Luton Grammar School), F.M.King (Assistant Master, Winchester College) and James himself. The author is extremely grateful to Rachel Neale, Archivist to the School, for her help in researching James' High Mastership.

[61]   Winchester College Archives, Annual Reports of the Headmaster to the Warden and Fellows (the Governing Body). These reports of the year's college activities also contain a section by Leeson on the national debate on educational issues during the war. It was a practice continued later by James in his own annual reports to the Governors of Manchester Grammar School. For this comment see Annual Report 1945.

[62]   M.G.S. Archives, Leeson notes on headmastership, a digest of which appear in anon, *Spencer Leeson: A Memoir*, (1958).

[63]   For Morse's comment, conversation with the author 1/April /2013.

[64]   M.G.S. archives. Much of the material supporting this section is derived from the minutes of the Governors' Meetings. They are a record of the regular work of the school but also include an annual report from the High Master. Relatively short documents, James added a brief section to his reports on the wider developments in education during the years from 1945-1961. For instance, each annual report contained the numbers of students winning Scholarships to university. Thus in 1934-5, the High Master Douglas Miller, reported 29 open scholarships to Oxford, Cambridge, Manchester and other universities, 33 local authority scholarships, six state scholarships, two Kitchener scholarships and also that 22 former pupils had gained first class honours degrees at Oxford and Cambridge. By 1943-4 that overall total had risen to 94. In 1945 it was already a very successful academic school.

[65]   J.L. Paton (1863-1946), High Master of Manchester Grammar School, 1902-1924.

[66]   M.G.S. archives, Governors' Minutes High Master's Annual Report (16 July 1946) on the anticipated impact of the direct grant system on the School with larger numbers staying on at school with the ambition to go to university, requiring staff changes to reflect this along with more laboratory and library facilities. James comments that the next five years *'will present a most interesting and challenging prospect …. and I feel that this school has a great responsibility to fulfil'* (author's emphasis).

[67]   M.G.S. archives: Governors' Minutes High Master's Annual Report (10 July

1956) reporting 50 State Scholarships won and 43 Open Awards at Oxford
and Cambridge. In 1955 101 boys left to study science and engineering.
In his Annual Report the following year, James commented that 75% of
pupils were now going to university, with the school gaining more awards to
universities than any other school in the country.

68   M.G.S. archives, Manuscript of Spencer Leeson's advice to a newly
      appointed headmaster.

69   J.A. Graham and B.A.Phythian (eds.), *Manchester Grammar School*, pp.123.

70   Roger Young Memorial Address 5/10/92 by permission of Professor Oliver
      James. Dr Ivan Hall, the architectural historian, and already a pupil at the
      school in 1945, thought him impressive and generous, but insensitive in his
      handling of some of the talented long serving staff. Interviewed by the author
      May 2014.

71   Michael R. Lee, *Stood on the Shoulders of Giants: A Medical Odyssey*
      (Spennymoor, County Durham, 2003), p.49.

72   Alan Garner, obituary tribute, *Ulula* (1992), see Appendix 5.

73   Author's interview with A.O.J. Cockshutt, 3 May 2013.

74   Stuart Sutcliffe Interviews, UoY/His/3/1/9.

75   M.G.S. Archives, Minutes of Governors, 26 Sept 1944, 17 Apr 1945, 17
      July 1945. M.G.S. had decided to be part of the direct grant grammar school
      scheme, whereby they agreed that up to one third of its places at 11 would be
      reserved for the local authority scholarships. M.G.S. formally accepted the
      government's regulations the following July and also later agreed to extend
      the catchment area to include Oldham, Lancashire, Cheshire and Derbyshire
      in addition to Manchester, thereby creating a large pool of potentially
      qualified boys to choose from.

76   His phrase the lottery of geography or money was regularly used. For his
      most explicit and vigorous justification, see Appendix 3.

77   M.G.S. Archives, Minutes of Governors 22 Apr1947, 20 Jan 1948.

78   The Hugh Oldham Boys' Club closed in 1958, see Nigel Watson, *MGS : a
      history at 500*, Manchester, 2015, p.126. On establishing the Services Group,

see Eric's Farewell Address to the School, BIA, UoY/JAM/1/1/1.

[79]   For the range of Eric's external activity see his Scripts, Speeches and
Lectures, 1940-1962, BIA, UoY/JAM/1/1/1. See also Eric James, *An Essay
on the Content of Education*, (London, 1949), *Education and Leadership*
(London, 1951).

[80]   For examples on educational themes see BIA, UOY/ JAM/1/1/1:' The Direct
Grant System' (n.d. late 1950s), 'Education and Industry: A Schoolmaster's
View' (n.d. c.1960)], Science and Religion (n.d.),' The Education of the
Scientist', (n.d.), 'The Education of Gifted Children' (n.d.).

[81]   Eric James, 'Crisis in Education: Grammar Schools in Danger', 'What shall
we teach?', 'Schools and the Home', *Sunday Times*, 17, 24, 31 Jan 1954.

[82]   For James' vigorous defence of the grammar school and hostility to the
Labour party's increasing support for universal comprehensive schools, see
his address to the Lancashire and Cheshire heads meeting in October 1954
in Appendix 3. For Gaitskell's reactions to the speech see Philip Williams
(ed.), *The Diary of Hugh Gaitskell, 1945-1956*, (London, 1983), pp. 338-9,
see appendix 4. For a broader treatment of the changing emphasis in the
education policy of the Labour Party, see Michael Parkinson, *The Labour
Party and the Organisation of Secondary Education, 1918-65*, (London,
1970).

[83]   James' commitment to the direct grant system as part of the state's provision
led him to decline the invitation to become headmaster of Winchester in
1954. See comment on James by R.N.Heaton, Deputy Secretary at the
Department of Education, James family papers. Confirmed by Professor
Oliver James 18/10/2015.

[84]   M.G.S. Archives, Minutes of Governors 10 July 1951, High Master's Annual
Report following the recent HMI inspection. 'My only serious criticism of
the report is its failure to acknowledge the social context within which the
school operates. It is simply not financially possible to have facilities as
comprehensive as public schools. This is one of the state's schools, run on
a budget determined by the state and with financial resources a fraction of
independent schools. Also pupils come from modest backgrounds for whom
practical issues of employability and skills are real. This has an impact on
what education is appropriate, given that a large numbers of the relatively
wealthy do not gain admission to the school'.

85   For Eric's views on education more broadly at this time, see his contributions
      to House of Lords debates: *Hansard*, 5th ser., vol.222 (23/3/60), col. 187, on
      the Crowther Report, vol.220 (9/12/59), col.225, on Science in Civil Life,
      vol.223, (11/5/60), col.682, on Lord Simon's motion that the government set
      up an enquiry into full time education after 18, vol.226 (29/11/60), col.1058,
      on Modern Aids in Education, vol.252 (24/7/63), col. 772.

86   See Michael Parkinson, *The Labour Party*. For the increasing polarisation
      of the education debate, see Gary McCulloch, *Philosophers and Kings:
      Education for Leadership in Modern England*, (Cambridge, 1991), pp. 66-81.

87   This is a persistently expressed difficulty in Eric's reports to the Governors,
      see M.G.S. Archives, Governors' Minutes 22 Apr 1947, 20 July 1948.

88   As early as 1950 M.G.S. governors were being challenged by Lady Simon
      of Wythenshawe on the school's policy of admission simply on academic
      merit and backing the High Master, M.G.S. archives, Governors' Minutes
      Oct 1950. It is worth recording that although divided on the question of
      comprehensive schools, the Jameses remained good friends of Lady Simon.

89   Stuart Sutcliffe Interviews, BIA/UoY/His/3/1/9.

90   See collection of testimonies to James from Robert Birley, headmaster
      of Eton, Sir George Pickering, R.N.Heaton and others on his leaving
      Manchester Grammar School by permission of Professor Oliver James.

91   For the Interim Report: TNA, UGC1/9 (9/3/61) and BIA, UoY/F/YUPC/3/10.
      On relations between Robbins and James, see James' written and oral
      accounts outlined in footnote 3 above.

92   The Robbins Report on Higher Education was the result of the changes in
      government thinking about student numbers in the late 1950s and of which
      the new universities were the result. The Robbins committee established
      in 1961, reporting in October 1963, the month that the University of York
      received its first students, was concerned with future projections of the
      numbers of undergraduate students.

93   Stuart Sutcliffe Interviews, BIA/ UoY/His/3/1/9, in which James comments
      that he did not share equally Robbins' enthusiasm for the Scottish degree
      structure,

94   BIA, The Rowntree Foundation Archive, Minutes of the Joseph Rowntree
      Memorial Trust, 30 Sept 1959.

95   For instance, Wallace submitted a memorandum to the Academic Planning
      Board on 14 Nov 1960 on the structure of the Social Sciences at York prior to
      any appointment of a vice-chancellor, York Minster Archives, Milner White
      Papers, IV/1.

96   On the appointment of Professor Alan Peacock, which came with Robbins'
      enthusiastic endorsement, see UoM Archives, Mansfield Cooper MS,
      VCA/7/206-York, Robbins to Mansfield Cooper, 28/7/1961. On the slightly
      surreal meeting first meeting of the two men see Alan Peacock, 'Very Early
      Days at the University of York', (typescript written 1996-7) by courtesy of
      David Foster, former Registrar of the University of York.

97   For James accounts of democratic structures see Stuart Sutcliffe Interviews,
      BIA/ UoY/His/3/1/9. It is also important to note that this more democratic
      structure of academic governance was initiated, not by Eric, but by the
      Academic Planning Board in a paper written by its vice-chairman, Sir
      William Mansfield Cooper, a few weeks after the Board's first meeting in
      December 1960. It is an example of the UGC's general desire to use the
      opportunity of new universities to push reform by example among existing
      universities, ironically, like Manchester, of which Mansfield Cooper was
      Vice-Chancellor. Manchester University Archives, Mansfield Cooper MS,
      VCA/7/266-York, Memo by Mansfield Cooper for Robbins on how the
      university's governance might be constructed to give non-professorial staff a
      greater role in general policy making. In the later discussions of the Charter
      and Statutes over what became subsequently the Professorial Board and
      the General Academic Board, Eric and his early academic appointees were
      concerned that there was a danger that, as drafted, the regulations would
      lead too frequently to stand-offs between the two bodies and that decisions
      on routine academic matters would be taken inappropriately by the Council.
      The Academic Planning Board was not persuaded and so the authority of
      the General Academic Board was re-affirmed. In practice, James and his
      colleagues' fears of excessive academic interference by the Council on
      constitutional grounds were not realised, enabling Eric to make the later
      positive comments on how the system as it had worked in practice.

98   On the origins of the idea of a collegiate university see John West-Taylor's
      briefing notes for delegates attending the Bishopthorpe meeting, 24 June
      1959 and his notes following the meeting, same date, BIA, UoY/YAT/MIN/1-
      7, UoY/F/YUPC/1/3. A collegiate model is not suggested in either set of
      notes.

99   For the development of the collegiate structure see Andrew Saint recordings

especially Nuttgens and Derbyshire, BL, Andrew Saint recordings in footnote
3 above.

[100]   The All Souls Group was an important, informal of group of those involved
in the strategic direction of education during and after World War II.
Founded by Dr. W.S.G. Adams, Warden of All Souls' College, Oxford in
1941, it met usually twice yearly in various Oxford colleges and heard and
discussed papers. Eric James addressed the Group in October 1948 on the
theme, 'What is an educated man in contemporary society?' He became a
member of the Group. Other members in 1959, who had some influence on
the founding shape and character of the University of York, include Henry
Morris (formerly Chief Education Officer for Cambridgeshire), Harry Rée
(then Headmaster of Watford Grammar School and later founding Head of
the Education Department, University of York), Norman Fisher (formerly
a colleague of Morris' in Cambridgeshire, Chief Education Officer of
Manchester City Council and in 1959 Principal of the Staff College of the
Coal Board) and Lady Ogilvie (Principal of St Anne's College, Oxford
and member of the University of York's Academic Planning Board), John
Newsom (Chief Education Officer for Hertfordshire from 1940 until 1957,
contemporary of Eric's at Queen's College, Oxford and described by him
as a life-long friend, who was also strongly influenced by Henry Morris and
Stirrat Johnson-Marshall) and Evelyn Sharpe (Permanent Secretary at the
Ministry of Housing and Local Government). Douglas Jay and Roy Jenkins,
then rising members of the Labour Party, were also members. For records
of the Group see University of London, Institute of Education Archives,
GB/366/DC/ASG.

[101]   For the process of appointing architects and his recommendation of Robert
Matthew Johnson-Marshall see Memorandum by John West-Taylor to the
Promotion Committee , nd. February 1961, BIA, UoY/F/YUPC/1/1. The
formal appointment of RMJM as 'development' architects 17 April 1961,
BIA, UoY/F/YUPC/1/1. The appointment was to produce the University
Development Plan in the first instance. Following the preparation and
acceptance of the Development Plan in April 1962, RMJM were re-appointed
as architects for phase 2 of the Development Plan (the first two colleges, the
first science complex and the creation of the 'balancing' reservoir in order to
drain the site). The conservation architect Bernard Feilden (1919-2018) had
the responsibility for the work on Heslington Hall, the Kings' Manor and the
other historic buildings acquired as part of the city's support for the fledgling
university

[102]   See BIA, UoY/F/YUPC/1/2 Promotion Committee Minutes 16/5/62 in

relation to UGC funding prior to the admission of the first students in October 1963. Broadly speaking, the UGC declined to make any contribution to the capital costs of the accommodation within colleges and would not make additional funds available until the first students had been admitted; in short, the University had to rely on its own resources for the next eighteen months.

[103] CLASP is the acronym for Consortium of Local Authorities Special Programmes, a system developed in response to the rapid expansion of newly constructed public buildings in the period.

[104] See BL, Andrew Saint Recordings in footnote 3 above.

[105] For the early discussions on academic, collegiate and departmental matters see notes on academic staff meeting 1962-3, BIA, UoY/F/ST. The decision on mixed colleges was made on 25 Aug 1962.

[106] The idea for a Languages Department was originally suggested by the mathematician, Sir William Hodge, Master of Pembroke College, Cambridge and a member of York Academic Planning Board.

[107] For the evolution of the academic structure of the University, see UGC discussion of the Interim Report of the Academic Planning Board, 9 Mar 1961, TNA, UGC1/9/1961 (9/3/61) and later discussions among the early academic appointments: BIA, UoY/F/ST.

[108] See Mark Williamson and David White, eds., *A History of the first fifty years of Biology at York*, (York, 2013). The author has also had the benefit of conversations about the founding of the Chemistry Department with Professor David Waddington.

[109] Stuart Sutcliffe interviews, BIA, UoY/His/3/1/9.

[110] Harry Rée and Eric Hawkins interviews, BIA, UoY/HIST/3/1/3, 4.

[111] Robbins had sounded out Peacock before he had met Eric and also was a referee for Douglas Dosser and Jack Wiseman in their applications to York. London School of Economics Archives, Robbins Ms/35, 39.

[112] The breakup of the Social Sciences part 1 curriculum occurred progressively over the years immediately following Eric's retirement. Information from Dr. David Foster, former Registrar.

113   On Tony Banks (later Lord Stratford) see James Merrill, 'Tony Banks from
       Campus to Cabinet', *Nouse* (a University of York student newspaper),
       30/1/2006. Eric always referred to himself as left of centre, as would not be
       wholly surprising given his provincial, nonconformist background. While
       the general re-organisation of secondary schooling and the abolition of the
       grammar school moved Eric away from an earlier reformism, he remained
       liberal on many social issues as he expressed in debates in the House of Lords
       on corporal punishment, homosexual law reform, juvenile punishment and
       developmental youth work. Cordelia was extremely active in juvenile justice
       and was later a member of the Seebohm Committee on Social Services, set
       up by the government in 1965.

114   Christopher Perry to the author by email, 9/2/2013.

115   For the comments of student journalists, see *Nouse*, 2/3/1967.

116   Ironically, Bloody Sunday occurred just after the publication first of the two
       editions in the spring term 1972. By the time of the second edition, late in
       term, it was old news and did not feature.

117   *Hansard*, 5th ser., Lords, vol. 293 (19/6/1968) col.547 on a debate on
       University Student Discontents; vol. 301, col.462 (23/4/1969) on a debate on
       Student Participation in Higher Education.

118   Conversation with Mr. John Yeomans, the solicitor in question, with the
       author, September 2015.

119   *Hansard*, 5th ser., Lords, vol.252, (24/7/1963) cols. 772(James), 782
       (Wootton), in a debate initiated by Lord Longford, Leader of the Labour
       Party in the Lords, on educational policies, in which he makes a wide-ranging
       statement on what a future Labour government would do in secondary
       education, with the focus on the abolition of selection at 11 and the general
       re-organisation of schools on comprehensive, non-selective lines. The two
       sides of the argument were well expressed by the contributions of Lord James
       and Baroness Wootton. It is worth noting that James and Wootton were long-
       standing friends and Baroness Wootton was one the first cohort of honorary
       graduands at the University of York. For a later contribution to the debate on
       non-selective secondary education in 1965, after the formation of the Labour
       government of Harold Wilson in October 1964, see *Hansard*, 5th ser., Lords,
       vol. 263, col. 183 (10/2/1965).

120   Roger Young's Memorial Address, 5 October 1992 by kind permission of
       Professor Oliver James.

[121] Speech by the Chancellor, Lord Clark, on Degree Day, 13 July 1973, on Lord James's retirement, by permission of Professor Oliver James.

[122] BIA, UoY/JAM/1/1/2. In manuscript with corrections.

[123] J.D.Bernal and Lancelot Hogben were leading British scientists before and after the Second World War who combined research distinction with a commitment to popularising the role of scientific research in human improvement. Their influence clearly informs Eric's thinking in this talk.

[124] Almost certainly Francis Hill, also an assistant master at Winchester and in 1945 the other Winchester short-listed candidate for the High Mastership at Manchester Grammar School.

[125] W.R.Inge, Dean of St Pauls and popular writer on church, religious, social and moral affairs between the Wars.

[126] R.G. Collingwood, idealist philosopher and historian of Roman Britain.

[127] Word unclear.

[128] The Bishop of Ripon was Geoffrey Lunt: *The Times,* obituary 18/11/1948 p.6

[129] Declamatory 'mark you' in text.

[130] Alfred Zimmern, academic scholar and popular writer on international affairs between the Wars. Charles Gore, liberal catholic Anglican priest, writer and Bishop of Birmingham and Oxford.

[131] Sentence unclear.

[132] Letter by kind permission of Professor Oliver James. The letter bears no address, either of sender or recipient.

[133] Arthur Deakin (1890-1955) – General Secretary of the Transport and General Workers Union.

[134] Sir Waldron Smithers (1880-1954) – Long serving Conservative Member of Parliament.

[135] The think tank Political and Economic Planning later became the Policy

Studies Institute in 1978.

136   This employers' organisation subsequently became the Confederation of
        British Industry in 1965.

137   Philip Williams (ed.), *The Diary of Hugh Gaitskell 1945-1956*, (London,
        1983), pp.338-9.

138   The position is High Master.

139   *Ulula* (1992).

140   Kendal Milne, a Manchester department store.

141   York Minster, Milner-White Ms IV.

142   See Robbins correspondence with Mansfield Cooper, July to December 1960,
        UofM Archives, Mansfield Cooper Ms, VCA/7/266-York. Mansfield Cooper
        was vice chancellor of Manchester University.

143   For the formation of the Academic Planning Board see TNA, UGC 1/8 (1960).

144   TNA, UGC 1/8 (1960).

145   TNA, UGC 1/8 (1960).

146   John West-Taylor left the meeting for this item.

147   In the notes of the interview with John West-Taylor, Christopher Storm-Clark
        records him saying that there were two candidates, one being favoured by
        Robbins. But it is reasonably clear that the committee wished to see if James
        would accept. It is not known who was also in Robbins' mind. BIA, UoY
        PP2/1.

148   Exact date not known.

149   Personal information

150   See footnote 4 above.

151   The list is the author's edited version of the original text. He has reproduced
        the name as in the original and added details to clarify the name of the person

(including initials if preceding the one cited and shortened names if widely used at the time). In the original document, dated 3 November 1960, each person listed has a brief CV attached. These CVs do not seem to have been prepared by the person submitting the name, but would appear to have drawn up by the administrator/secretary preparing the paper for the committee from that year's *Who's Who*. The author has edited these entries, so that the person's position in 1960 is the only one given in the majority of cases as well as their dates of birth and death to aid those seeking further biographical information. In addition, in the surviving carbon copy in the Mansfield Cooper papers, some manuscript additions have been made (presumably by Mansfield Cooper himself) adding the names of those persons who had nominated the suggested individual, or on one or two occasions, a personal comment. There are relatively few of these manuscript additions, but in the case of James there is a name and it is Wallace.

[152]   Raymond Charles Smail (1913-1986), medieval historian of the Crusades and Fellow of Sidney Sussex, Cambridge and Chairman of the History Faculty Board, active in the Workers Educational Association.